FROM THE UV FILES

Underground Voices

http://www.undergroundvoices.com

Edited by Cetywa Powell

© 2012 by Underground Voices
All rights reserved.

ISBN: 978-0-9830456-3-2

Printed in the United States of America.

FILE NUMBERS

FICTION
Steven Loton	File #5
William C. Kilby	File #17
D. Keramitas	File #22
Daniel Davis	File #37
William J. Fedigan	File #50
Phillip Gardner	File #58
Gary Clifton	File #77
Nick Medina	File #80
Jo Neace Krause	File #92
Christian Riley	File #101
Beau Johnson	File #107
Timothy Bearly	File #121
TT Jax	File #127
Scott Neuffer	File #136
Ellen Denton	File #149

POETRY
Ken Poyner	File #13
Riley Spilman	File #33
Steven Gulvezan	File #47
Cassandra Dallett	File #96
Sara Letourneau	File #99
Jonathan Hine	File #118
Mary Shanley	File #132
Ron D'Alena	File #133
Catfish McDaris	File #148

CONTRIBUTORS BIOS — **159**

From the UV Files

File #5
STEVEN LOTON

The Gun

Harry had a gun. But he had no bullets. So he kept the gun in his top drawer. He only took it out when he got drunk. He would take it out, wave it in the air, point it, aim it, look in the mirror and scream all sorts of tough guy talk. Mostly it was nonsense. Soon that got boring so he would shove it down his pants and just stand there looking in the mirror pretending to actually be a tough guy. More nonsense and that got shit too so he would just go back to the bottle. Harry never got tired of that. That was great.

After another ball busting fight with Jessica, Harry thought, God damn this, I'm taking my gun and I'm going to the bank.

"Darling," said Jessica, "you are the dumbest sack of shit I have ever come across. No bank is open at ten pm."

Harry checked his watch. She was right. It was 10pm. But Harry couldn't stand for that sort of lip. He had that all day long from the boss. He didn't want to come home and hear it too.

"What about bars ha, are they open at ten pm?" Harry enquired.

"Yes Harry, they are. But they are full of witnesses. Do you know what witnesses are?"

"Huh?"

"Look Harry, pass me that nail polish."

Harry went to her makeup bag, emptied it. A whole bunch of crap fell out. He got the polish and threw it over. It landed nowhere near her.

"How much do I pay for all this crap?" He was rifling through her drawers. Then he pulled her panties out. "These. Do you really need these? We could be rich if you didn't spend my money on useless clothing."

Then he had Jessica's work shoes. He was holding them above his head. They hung. "And these, what about these?"

Jessica sighed and carried on painting her nails. She was lying in bed. The pillow propped her head up and she was wearing her fluffy night gown. The white one. Her favourite. Harry liked her to sleep naked. Or naked, but with stockings on. But Harry was usually drunk and forgot what she was wearing.

"Listen baby, one day I'll make it. I swear I'm the greatest driver in the company. Soon, I'll be the boss. Then I'll be on double what I make now. We'll be rich baby."

Her nails were painted bright red and she was reading Huxley.

"Say something then."

She looked up, blinked. "Harry you have been in that job for six years now. The only thing that has happened was the demotion last year. You got ducked wages and then fired. I had to write a letter pleading for your job back. I was amazed they gave it back."

She blew on her nails.

"But baby that wasn't my fault. You know they were on my back. They were scared. I was moving up too fast. That's the way it goes in the work force. The boss man doesn't like to see workers succeed. They don't want us to fail either. They just want us to stay still forever. It keeps society in check. Don't you understand that baby?"

Harry had his shirt off and was flexing in the mirror. He wasn't much of a man but at least he liked what he saw. He used to be muscled and tanned. But he couldn't keep up with that game. The gym was for wimps. All that grunting. He got sick of it. Now he was a real man with a real job. Driving trucks. Or sometimes loading trucks. But if he had his way, it would just be driving trucks. Harry turned the gun, pointing the barrel toward his face, and looked into it.

"Baby, have you been playing with my gun? It looks like someone has been playing with it. Or maybe you were just cleaning it for me. Were you cleaning Daddy's gun?"

"No Harry, I haven't touched your gun. I don't know why you have that thing. It doesn't even work."

"Oh it works. I can prove it. Look." He was pulling the trigger. It went click, click, click. "Hear baby. Hear that. That's a real gun."

He stood there pulling the trigger, grinning like a moron. Or a subnormal. A subnormal moron.

"I could hold up a bank with this. At least a small shop."

"Look Harry," She slammed Huxley down and rose up

from the bed. "Why don't you then? You're always talking about it. But that's all. You are the biggest chicken shit I have ever been with. Maybe I should go back to Mike. He talked big but at least he backed it up."

"You think I won't do it." He pulled on a white T-shirt on and climbed into his favourite pair of denim blue jeans. They really were disgraceful looking jeans.

"I'll do it. I'll rob a bank, or a shop, or an off-licence. I don't give a damn. I'll even rob an old lady. I'll do it."

"You fool."

She slid back into bed and pulled her eye mask down. That usually meant she didn't want to talk anymore. Then she reached and pulled the cord on the lamp. It went dark.

That was it. Harry had enough of this. On the way out he was sure to take his gun. No point in forgetting that. He opened the door, slipped out and sure did slam it. He had to let Jessica know how angry he was. He let the whole building know.

His car was still parked out front. Hadn't been touched. Not even the thieves wanted it. Piece of crap. He got in and started ripping up the engine. A cloud of smoke poured out of the exhaust. He really had to get that seen to. He fiddled with his gun, twisting the barrel like they did in the movies and thought about that for a while. A few minutes passed and nothing came to him so that was enough of that.

Harry put it into first gear and took off. Just him and the open road. Man was born to drive alone. He snapped on the radio. Pop music. No luck. He fiddled with the dial. It set. Rolling Stones. Gimme Shelter. Jagger ha. That skinny bastard. That'll do, that'll do. He drove it steady along the grey road. There seemed to be no one about so Harry opened the valves up, tore along with the window down and his arm hanging out. Some breeze blew his hair wildly. Just like in the movies. He couldn't see shit. Then he saw what he wanted. A bar. He parked it across the street and sat there. Then he turned the engine off real slow. He didn't know what he was doing. In fact he felt very stupid just sitting there. Man spent so much of their life seeking solitude. When they finally had some they had no idea what to do with it. He should write that down, maybe. Later. He had more important things to do.

The gun was in the glove box. Harry took it out. He got out

of the car and tucked the piece away down the back of his jeans. He sprinted across the street, opened the door, walked in and sat down. He kept his head low. Finally he looked up. Nice place, respectable people. Some were even seated at the restaurant area. He counted two waitresses, but no bar man. Then he appeared. How could Harry miss him? He was about the ugliest son of a bitch Harry had ever seen. Or anyone had ever seen.

"Whadyah want friend? Want food? I'm the chef too. Names Bill."

Jesus.

"No thanks Bill. Just a beer please. Maybe in a glass, if it's no bother."

He poured it from the tap and set it down. Harry grabbed the handle, brought it up and took a large gulp.

"Drinking alone?" Bill asked. "Had a fight with the lady? Or you got no lady?"

He released a laugh and all of his body parts wobbled and continued to wobble.

"Oh he's a ladies' man," said the old guy two stools up. "I can tell. Isn't that right Rich?"

Then Rich joined in. Another loner.

"I don't know. I haven't had a woman in years. I can never tell. I'm sure he does better than me, but that won't make him a ladies' man. Ah hell, I need another piss."

Bill hammered his palm down on the wood. The ashtray bounced up. There was some silence. They all looked or twitched. "Piss or shit Rich? You already clogged that toilet up once. You don't wanna have to clean it up again now, DO YOU?"

Rich just sat there staring into his drink and blinking. Bill wiped along the wood until he reached Harry. Harry raised his beer. Bill wiped under it.

"Another one?"

Harry nodded.

"You a sports man, friend? We love sports here. That's all we talk about."

"Women too," said Rich. "We talk about women."

Just then door the opened. It flew open. Two men ran in. They wore all black and had stockings covering their heads. Both had guns. They were flashing them too. Every one hit the deck.

Harry was last to.

"WE WANT THE CASH. ALL OF IT. NOW EMPTY THE TILL FAT BOY."

He was talking to Bill, but Bill had trouble getting to his feet. Finally he did and opened the till. Bill was clawing at the notes. He was sweating, scared. The taller man hopped over the bar, pushed Bill over and started to empty cash. He was shoving all the notes into his pockets. Didn't look like much. Bill was on the floor breathing heavily.

"YOU LOOKING AT SOMETHING, OLD MAN? I MEAN, VERY OLD MAN?"

The shorter of the two was talking to Rich. Rich looked up, damn near shit himself, said, "No sir, no I swear I'm not."

"Good." He adjusted the stocking on his head. That was better. "NOW EVERYONE THROW THE WALLETS AND PURSES AND ANY OTHER VALUABLES ONTO THE FLOOR. DON'T BE SHY."

Nobody moved.

"NOW."

Everybody moved. All the wallets and purses were out. There was even some jewelry thrown down.

One fat balding lady began the family talk.

"Please don't hurt me. I got a son. A handsome son. Look." She flashed a photo of her six-year old boy. Ugly looking thing. "Please. And here's my husband. A great man. Look." She had a photo of him too. She held it up and showed all of us. Pops was no looker. The kid had no hope.

"Harold," said the short one. "Come and look at this one. She's just how you like 'em. Fat."

Harold raised his head, stood up, kicked somebody in the gut, jumped the bar and walked over, slowly.

"Did you say my name?"

"I'm sorry Harold, I'm sorry. I get nervous."

"Relax. Where's this bitch?"

"There. Look." He pointed. She was really weeping, but now she had all the family photos out, flashing them around.

Harold eyed her. He liked it. Then he mounted her. He used his hands to work her legs open. He got his pants down. She didn't even struggle.

Harry saw it. He had a raging feeling inside. Guess it was anger. Or maybe hunger. No, it was definitely anger. He hadn't felt it in years. He felt alive. Like a powerful creature. He couldn't stand for this. Jesus, he couldn't stand for this. He stood up and walked toward the bar, stepping over people. A half-drank beer was sitting there. He picked it up and belted it back.

The short fat one saw. "Harold, look." He pointed at Harry. Harold hadn't even started working away yet so he climbed off, fuming.

"What's this shit, tough boy. You wanna get blown away eh? Like bye bye." Harold waved.

Then Harry took his glass, stretched over the bar, grabbed the beer tap and pulled it. Beer poured out. Harry filled up. He took a good gulp then nodded to the lady.

"Get up."

She gathered up her family photos, her bag, her fake pearls, her life, everything. She was up.

"That's a silly mistake," said Harold. He levelled his pistol at Harry. The shorter crook didn't know what the hell was happening.

"Don't be stupid man. We got the money and wallets. Let's get the hell outer here."

"Shut up Geoffrey."

"Oh shit, oh shit, you said my name. I don't wanna go to jail man."

Harry finished his drink. He put the glass down then slowly reached. He pulled his gun out and let it hang to one side of his body. It felt good that way. Nonchalant. Like in the movies.

"Look Harold, he has a gun. Oh shit we're in trouble now. He looks nuts too. Maybe he's police. You police sir?"

Harold slapped Geoffrey hard. "I said shut your hole."

Then he ripped Geoffrey's stocking off and threw it to the ground. Geoff dived for it. Too late.

"Oh shit, oh shit. They saw my face."

It was true. Everyone did. And it really shook up the old couple huddled in the corner. Geoffrey had red hair, slim lips, only a few teeth and the palest blue eyes. His facial features indicated that he had never had a woman in his whole life. Or even a man. He quickly pulled the stocking back on.

"Now, I'm going to count to three," said Harry "If you're

still standing there, I'll have to let off a few rounds. But I'm a kind man so I'll count slowly. One...."

Harold laughed. Geoffrey panicked.

"Come on Harold. We got the cash and wallets. Let's go."

"Two..."

"All right tough guy. We'll go. But I'm taking her with me." He pointed out fatso. She was already screaming but she took it up a notch. She was very loud.

"No can do, Harold," said Harry "Now, scram, before I reach three."

Geoffrey backed out first. He kept pointing his piece. Harold followed. Then they were gone.

Harry went to the tap and poured another beer. People started to stand up. Some slowly, others helping. There were hugs and handshakes going on. Suddenly everyone was smiling. They all felt alive again. Some would go home and make drastic plans to change their lives. But nothing would ever come of it. Harry just drank his beer off.

Then he heard the police sirens in the distance. They were too late as usual.

Fatso approached Harry. "Thank you sir."

"Harry."

"Thanks Harry. My son thanks you too. Here look." She flashed the picture at Harry.

"Yeah, yeah okay lady, put it away now."

"Listen," said Bill, "Police are here. You got a gun too. You better get the hell out of here. Go."

Harry looked around. Everyone was nodding. They all had tears in their eyes. Then Rich pointed to the back. "Go that way."

Harry finished his beer, got up and walked toward the exit. Then he stopped, turned and looked at the gun. It was sitting on the bar. He blinked, turned and was gone. Gun in hand.

Harry got into his car and sat there. He wasn't in shock. He put the key in and jacked up the engine. He drove off slowly. Two police cars came racing toward him. They flew past. He checked the rear-view mirror. Their flashing lights disappeared into the night. Harry drove along like a good citizen.

When Harry got home, Jessica was sleeping in her white night gown. Harry took his T-shirt off, those jeans and climbed in,

From the UV Files

slowly, so not to wake her.

Then Harry wrapped his arm around her, pulled her in close and smelled her hair. Like strawberries it was. They slept.

From the UV Files

File# 13
KEN POYNER

Field Work

Go to the touristy place
With the strings of shells
Hanging at every corner of the
Inescapable roof. Inside,
One of several seeming locals
Will sell you shirts and plastic fish
And that bubble gum you haven't seen
Any place else. A woman
Who should not be wearing
A bikini top and shorts
Will be sitting in a three legged chair,
Wearing a bikini top and shorts,
Angled against the thin wall:
Watching you.
Take your time at the postcards.
Keep the display case between
You and the sun bloodied front door.
In the back
At a bar with only four stools
A man will be leaning forward with no care
For the one drunk
Or alleged drunk
On the last stool on the left.
Making your way as slowly
As a stone crab ordering a cheeseburger
Edge to the bar. Place your arm
On the counter and sit
On the stool standing one seat in from the right.
When the barkeep leans your way
Asking what you will have,
Ask him if he knows me,
Has seen me nosing about,
Remembers the man in the short
But privileged Panama hat.

From the UV Files

If he says yes
Place two dollars face up on the bar,
Pat your pocket twice like a broken man,
And get out before the shooting starts.

From the UV Files

File# 15
KEN POYNER

The Objective of Torture

You may commit any atrocity,
Leave any mark, create
Any permanent infirmity,
As long as the information received
Is correct. You may use
Any tool, including those
Designed for butchering hogs
Or straightening a child's teeth.
Truth is the only end.
There are no off-limits places:
You can tweedledee this,
Tweedledum that,
Scorch what you like,
Cut off what is, in this context,
Currently effective. But
Your information has to be sound.
You can use external power sources –
Car batteries or the city electric grid,
Propane canisters, sterno,
Kerosene or even whale oil if you have it.
None of it matters except
The information must be accurate,
Timely and of use. Families
Are fair game. If places were changed
Families would be fair game.
The rose of a bruise,
A torn shirt, the sound
Of terror in another room
Reaching maturity, coming abloom.
Only: the information must be true.
But, sometimes
Our work is best when there is
Nothing to tell, and the lie
And truth settle down in the same bed

From the UV Files

And howl the same poem. Information
By degrees is overrated.
Feel for what is marrow in the heart.

From the UV Files

File #17
WILLIAM C. KILBY

Franklin St.
(for Heller)

It was a bum case. I knew that from the beginning, not that I had ever had a case before. Up until then, all Uncle Sam had ever asked me to do was to edit news copy coming back from Korea; but I knew what dead ends looked like.

When they called me to the general's office, when he wasn't there, I knew. Only me and a nameless man in plain clothes with loose ideas. At best, this was going to be busy work. At worst, it would be a suicide mission. Twelve senior officials incapacitated. No links. No leads. Just a file with the names and best guesses on current locations. Just the mystery man and me, a kid. A smart kid with a secret and two choices, take the case or face the court-martial. I didn't think then that he knew what to discharge me for, only that he would figure it out if he had to. I took the case, or whatever it was.

There was virtually nothing to go on outside of guesses, and in the Pentagon, in 1955, the best guess was always Russia. Some sort of super-weapon. Chemical, psychological maybe. Whatever it was, it was selective. Twelve men so far. Everyone a major player. I might not have been a real investigator, but I had read enough dime store novels to know not to guess without evidence so I started down my list.

General McLuhan, my former superior. Victim zero. Last known address 75 West Fourth Street. No answer at the door. I let myself in, called his name once or twice, then heard the creaking from the study. There he was, with six feet of finality tethering him to the rafters and the four legs of a stool laid down beneath. No smell. He hadn't been there long. Pants on. Belt buckled. No accident here. No games. Just a man, his rope and one less name on my list.

Phone it in. Close the door. Move on.

The next two names were easy enough to track down. They were sharing a room at the only place in town without an exit door. When Mr. No-name gave me this case, I wondered what exactly "incapacitation" meant. I was beginning to get the idea.

Why they even wasted a padded room on these two was beyond me. To say they were not violent would have been a joke. They were nearly catatonic, just sitting there. One Indian style, one with legs splayed out. Eyes glassy. Their lips were the only moving parts, but they were not moving well. A gear was slipping somewhere. Gibberish probably. A few repeated sounds. Jot it down. Could be Russian for all I know, but not likely. No one who talks like that could be considered a serious threat to the state.

No, I don't need to go in. I can see all I need to from the window. Just cross off two more names and turn away. Save the tears for when you get back to Franklin Street where boys are allowed to cry. Boys do a lot of things back there. The kinds of things that might make all this a little easier to handle; but they're also the kinds of things that get good soldiers court-marshaled, and I have work to do.

I praised god out loud when Secretary Haynes answered his door. Finally, a lead. A real person who would be able to tell me something. He motioned me inside with a hand that held a long, slender brush. There must have been a thousand of them in there. Paintings. Everywhere. They covered every wall in the old brownstone. They stood in high stacks in the hallway and on the furniture. They dangled precariously from every ledge. It was like one of those cautionary tales mothers tell their children. Now Johnny, if you don't clean your room, you'll end up like old Mr. Haynes, crushed in an avalanche of his paintings.

It might have been bearable if not for the singularity of the work. Blue orb, black slash through the center. Blue orb. Black slash. Over and over. Be cool. Don't spook him. Blue orb. He may be your only lead. Black slash.

"So you're a painter," I say but receive nothing.

"Come on man." I grab him. "Give me something." I shake him but there is nothing to be had. Only a vacant set of eyes and silence as he turns away, back to the painting.

Great. One corpse, two nuts and a mute. It might have made a fine joke had I been back at the Blind Pig with the boys, but I was right there in the middle of it, and it wasn't funny.

I packed up my worries and headed home. Past the Blind Pig. Past the festive awnings of Franklin Street. Up the stairs to my room. There would be no socializing tonight. These thoughts are not the kind you share. I'll see the mystery man again tomorrow. I'll run down a couple more leads. Maybe I'll have something to tell him.

New day. Up with the sun. I never could sleep in, even before all this. Shower, shave, and out the door, but it was no use. The leads were shit. Just two more bodies. A couple weeks ago they had been men of power and influence, world shapers. Now they were just bodies with nothing to say and nothing for me to tell mystery man.

There was time left in the day so I drove out to Fredericksburg for one last lead. Colonel James Randolph. Not a real Colonel, more of an honorary title. He had been to Germany, and Korea, and Cuba, unofficially of course. Now he was the President's right hand man, staring down the Russians and anyone else rude enough to challenge the state. I skipped ahead on the list to get to him. Too many bodies. I needed to see a living man. If he was half as tough as the talk about him, he would be my best shot.

I made the drive, but he wasn't there. Just the family. A wife. Two kids. He's lost his shit she says, and gets offended when I'm not surprised. Sorry lady, if you wanted surprise, you should've caught me yesterday. She says he's gone to their place in the city. They have a place in the city? A wasted drive. They had better comp my travel. But I don't have a travel account yet. More and more I think they don't expect me to claim anything, or to make it back at all.

A penthouse apartment, and it's on C Street. I could have walked. No answer. The door is locked. Kick it in. The lights are off, but I see him by the open window. Dress blues. I'm just in time for the show.

"Hold it," I yell and draw my pistol. Pull back the hammer. Play the badass. Hope he responds, but no, just laughter.

"I heard the new kid was green, but you're something else."

"Step away from the window sir."

"Sorry kid, but you're the one who needs to hold it. If you want me splattered on the sidewalk half dressed, take another step, and I'll oblige you. Otherwise, I'd like a moment to finish up with this brass."

"Fine Colonel, just tell me why. What happened to you?"

"Sorry kid. If you're lucky you'll never understand."
"But I can stop it, if you help me."
"Have you ever loved a good woman?"
"No."

"Good for you," he fixed his cufflinks. "Most kids your age can't think about anything else, but I'll tell you this. There is nothing special or impressive or noble about falling in love. Anybody can do it. It's as easy as quitting cigarettes or passing gas. The trick is hanging on, making it last." He fixed the last chevron. "We only get so many nights." He snugged his tie knot. "Don't spend any more alone than you have to." And he slipped out the window.

The last name on my list. The toughest man in uniform. A pile of guts on the street.

I went to the bar early and waited for the man without a name. Whiskey. Rocks. Dangerous thoughts. What was I going to say? What did he expect me to? Surely others before me had been assigned this, and surely they had failed. What happened to them? Are they on the list now?

I thought about the orb. The pale, icy blue orb and the black that divided it like a rift in the sea. I thought about Colonel Randolph. Whatever this thing was, it was big. Too big for me and probably for mystery man too. The others were pitiful and strange but they didn't hit me like Randolph. Maybe it was being there in the final moment. Maybe it was watching all that strength wash away. What the hell could do that? What could turn a man like that into a sappy old coot, rambling on about his family? What secret was he keeping?

It wouldn't matter. It wouldn't persuade my nameless commander. Succeed or fry. That much had been clear from the start. He wouldn't have to look hard for a reason to pin me. The eyes are always there to see and the lips there to speak. Even here they watch. They see. Screw them. I'll make my case and take my chances. It has to be better than this. I can't unsee the bodies, but I can sure as hell keep from seeing more.

"Who let you in here?" The words came softly from my right. "This is supposed to be a place for fun, but your heart is so heavy I can feel it from here."

A smart girl she was. Beautiful and exotic. Long and tender

with a hungry smile. Every man's dream, no doubt.

"I could help you lift it. That heart of yours. My room is just upstairs."

Scan the room. No sign of mystery man. Just the watchful eyes. If I'm going to face the court-martial, I'd better start building a defense. I follow her hips up the stairs and almost want to. There in the room, pressed together against the bar, I want to talk. She doesn't.

What about that accent? From a far away place that doesn't want her anymore, she says. I ask about her employer. She laughs and says that she makes her own hours. Then I see it. The black tress that falls against her pale blue eye. She pours the wine but I don't worry. There's nothing toxic, not in the bottle.

Clarity. In all of it. What Randolph was talking about. Who he was protecting. What the nameless man knew all along. Why I was chosen. The Russians didn't make anything. They just found it. Pushed it off on us as much to protect themselves as to do us any harm. Nothing here is new. It's the stuff myths were made of. Beauty, desire and the insatiable thirst. A natural weapon. More human than human. Too much to bear for those sad souls in the padded room, and those in the grave. Too much even for her I hope. Either way she won't have to go through it again.

She pulls me in, and I welcome the touch.

Press lips against lips and barrel against flesh. Squeeze the trigger and release the final breath.

"Why," she says slumping into my arms, the cold lovely eyes now shocked, maybe for the first time.

"Shhhh. It's okay now."

"Why don't you love me?"

"Shhh," I say again, "You can rest now."

"But they all love me."

"Baby, you're not the only one who's special."

I hold her close and feel her leave. Together we slide down to the floor. I lay her head on my chest and close my eyes. Franklin Street will still be there tomorrow. We both deserve some company tonight.

From the UV Files

File #22
D. KERAMITAS

Interesting Times

A car speeds into the mucky green of a scene viewed through an infrared lens. The armored BMW hurtles around, turns, replicating the curvy script of the local road signs. Two cars appear and flank the BMW, slowing it to a halt. Smudges in camouflage fatigues pull passengers from the vehicle and hurl them to the ground, make them lie with arms crossed behind their heads. A woman in a long dress is ordered into one of the battered cars. She throws off the hands of her assailants and flounces into the car, which speeds off as the night scene deepens, leaving a dark green limbo. The video image is replayed several times by a man in early middle age. The country is Bayon, where the man is on an overseas assignment for a large American corporation. The woman in the video is his wife.

"Pure luck that security camera was on," Coughlin tells him. "We thought of it, and there it was. Good thing we got it before the local law."

Coughlin is a kidnap consultant flown in from Singapore on a day's notice. Kidnap consultants are in demand in this part of the world, just as atrocity therapists, instability analysts, and disaster-preparedness trainers are popular elsewhere. They even advertise in the East Asia Review and Craig's List, but it was Coughlin who got in touch with him. Getting up to put on the lights, he looks bored.

"Haven't you had enough Mr. Leeming?"

Leeming can't get enough of the video. He's been married for eighteen years, travelled tens of thousands of frequent flier miles, moved from one place to another—30 moves—has gone through millions. All that, distilled into this grainy two-minute loop. He can't get enough, craving a clarity which is unavailable. But he knows Coughlin will think him odd, so he switches it off, gets up, and looks at the consultant.

"You think this video will provide you with some clues, Coughlin?"

"Oh, yes. Now I know who kidnapped your wife, and why."

Leeming sits back down heavily. He stares at the other man. Coughlin smiles.

From the UV Files

"First, let me congratulate you on having a wife with style."

*

The plainclothes policemen pop nuts and chatter amiably. Yet Leeming knows they're no different from the malevolent men in uniform who frame unfortunate souls at the airport for drug smuggling. He sits alone at a bare table, hands on the tabletop, sweating in spite of the overhead fan and noisy air conditioner, as if he were the criminal.

"This is all you know?" a policeman asks.

"Yes."

"Good. And you haven't seen your wife since?"

"Of course not."

"Good."

Technically, Leeming is now a sort of criminal. He's withholding evidence per Coughlin's orders. It's not sure the Ling organization is responsible for the kidnapping, but they have as many tentacles as the ruling family's holding companies. Some of the tentacles are in the police. Leeming wonders if that's a bad thing. Couldn't he take care of this on a transactional basis, like at work? If this is how things work here ...

The one named Tambol seems in charge, though (or because) he rarely says anything. He hangs back, staring with clinical contempt. Whether for Leeming or the other police isn't clear.

"Nothing else?" Tambol asks.

"No. Is that good?" says Leeming.

"Not very good. You are a person of interest."

"What does that mean?"

"You don't leave Bayon. We keep this."

Lieutenant Tambol takes the blue passport, and slips it in his right jacket pocket.

"I'm willing to cooperate," says Leeming. "I'll help with the expense involved. Whatever's in my wallet, just for starters."

Tambol removes the bills from Leemings's soft leather wallet.

"You like mushrooms, mistuh? Magic mushrooms open up head wide wide!" He's mocking, doing a parody of hustler pidgin. "Smoke some opium? Thai stick?"

Tambol bursts into a cackle. Leeming looks on with

disbelief but the other officers seem relieved. They escort him out of the room, into glutinous late-afternoon sunlight. On an impulse Leeming looks back to see the bills drop into a left jacket pocket.

*

Leeming recognizes the children as they shuffle through Arrivals. One of his assistants holds a sign reading LEEMING above his head. In a way, he doesn't recognize them—they seem shrunken, wizened, stricken. His stepchildren after a wasting illness, like those friends with AIDS back in the eighties. His two stepsons and stepdaughter huddle together as they walk, wheeling their luggage. They see the sign, then his face. He tries to smile.

"Hi, kids. How was your flight? No problem at customs, right? Grams and Gramps doing okay under the circumstances? You all hungry? You must be famished, right? You must be hungry, no?"

Leeming keeps the questions coming. He doesn't wait for answers. Actually, he dreads them. The children come out with their own questions, all about the whereabouts of their mother. Hesitantly, then with assurance, he handles one question after another.

"We know your Mom is in the country. There's no way she could leave. We know she's in good health, and based on past cases she's being kept under good conditions."

He's using crisis-management language. Part of him hates it, but he doesn't know what else to do. He realizes that this is effective with the kids. With pronounced authority he grabs the hand luggage, passing it to assistants and porters. With the gallant gestures he used to use with girlfriends, including his wife when he was single, he helps the children into the limo. Leeming bends over towards his oldest.

"XYZ," he says in a low, conspiratorial voice.

The boy smiles, and Leeming smiles back.

*

In Bayon City one lives and works on top of the world. Twenty, thirty, forty stories above the shantyscape. Above the smog, in golden sunlight, like Mount Olympus. Leeming knows the feeling of control that altitude gives is illusory. Still, exhilaration plays on his fingers as he spreads documents before the trustees. There are three trusts of which his wife is beneficiary. The trustees, who flew in overnight, are lawyers and longstanding friends of the family—her family. They are people who have often ignored him at formal and informal gatherings.

"It's at moments like these that funds should remain in the hands of professionals," says Fairly.

Oscar Fairly is the worst: he thinks control over the trust makes him some sort of surrogate father figure for Elaine.

"No," says Leeming. "I don't think so. That is, the trust deed doesn't say so."

He's referring to addenda, to the original document. In case of Elaine being in a coma, disabled, disappeared, or God forbid, dead, he, Leeming is to assume the role of protector overseeing the trustees and if necessary taking on functions normally reserved for said trustees. Leeming figures his children need continuity, not to mention those people whose livelihoods depend on the trusts. He might also need access to millions of dollars to pay a ransom, which the trustees might perversely refuse.

"An emergency use of important sums will have to be effected quickly, without time wasted on formalities."

He's astonished at how confidently he expresses himself. In the past he's only been capable of mumbles when obligated to make small talk with "the mandarins," as his wife called them. They are astonished, as well. Leeming has always been likeable and competent, within his own sphere, whether as spouse or middle manager. Coughlin, sitting in, seems self-satisfied, though he isn't directly concerned. He gets up the nerve to speak out.

"You know, if we have to put up a ransom it's only temporary. The money'll be recovered pronto. If anything, we have to keep an eye on the local police."

He smiles a broad smile with the discolored tint of old greenbacks. Coughlin doesn't inspire the same confidence with the lawyers that he does with Leeming. On the other hand, old Mr. Davis does inspire confidence, and trepidation. Though in a privileged position and well past the age of naked ambition, Davis snapped at the opportunity provided by Leeming's phone call.

"We have to respect the rules of the game," he says. "Even if the tenor of the game has changed. I fully support Mr. Leeming's assumption of the responsibility his wife intended he should have over her money."

"Her family's money," says Fairly.

"He is part of the family, Oscar," says Davis, looking over his glasses and down his long nose. "Unlike you."

*

"Is there any reason for him to be here?" says a project chief, indicating Coughlin.

Coughlin rises from his chair, discretion being a main ingredient of professionalism, but Leeming waves him back down.

"Sit, Mr. Coughlin. That's your seat."

Coughlin sits down sheepishly.

"Please don't think my wife's predicament is purely a personal matter. It concerns this company. It concerns security, and perceptions of security. That includes by the markets."

Leeming stands straight and talks evenly, though a tone or so higher than usual. It feels good to project oneself into responsibility. He hasn't had much opportunity for that in recent years.

"Mr. Leeming, I didn't mean to—"

"Hand me the insurance documents, please."

Leeming pretends to study them, having read the papers as soon as they came in.

"The policy does cover ransom—'return indemnification' they call it. The ransom is $8,000,000 and they'll pay it, but as with any policy there's a deductible: $800,000."

The managers say they will gladly pay to have Mrs. Leeming back safe and sound, which means they will gladly have the company pay. Leeming points out that if things go well the kidnappers won't keep their ransom very long. Then $75,000 for Coughlin won't seem so exorbitant.

"Plus expenses," says Coughlin, plainly speaking about money being another of his qualities.

"Both his fee and his expenses are deductible," adds the accounts man, trying to be helpful.

*

By the time the courier brings the parcel to Leeming, it's seeping. A crimson stain blooms on one side like a holiday decoration. Leeming takes the small parcel from the courier and looks at it curiously, but his hands immediately begin shaking so that he has to put it down on his desk. A pink film spreads from one corner onto the desktop, foaming slightly. He makes a call to Coughlin, who arrives a few minutes later.

"Do you know who sent it?" asks Coughlin.

"Anonymous sent it," says Leeming.

"Do you know what's in it?" Coughlin asks, like a doctor deliberately going through a list of symptoms.

"No. I haven't looked."

Coughlin lifts up the parcel and matter-of-factly rips off its paper surface.

"Well, let's see what's inside," he says.

There are sheets of toilet tissue inside the parcel which Coughlin pulls out. The first handfuls are light blue. Then bloodstained wads, like Kleenex that's been used on a nosebleed.

"My God," says Leeming, putting his face in his hands.

He's suddenly reminded of Elaine's miscarriages, all that blood.

"Tissue," says Coughlin picking at something in the box.

"More tissue paper?"

"Human tissue."

"What?"

"Could be anything. There's some bone or cartilage in it."

Leeming leaps up and paces around his desk with his hands still in his face, until Coughlin sits him down in a chair. It's the same chair Leeming had him sit in earlier. They both realize it; Coughlin remains grim-faced, but Leeming smiles at the irony. He sits up and has Coughlin take away "the forensic evidence."

*

Elaine's aunt and uncle, the ones who raised her, fly in, come to lend moral support.

"And simply to be near Elaine, wherever she might be in this godforsaken country!"

They are trust protectors, overseeing the trustees, with veto powers over actions affecting all funds. Unlike the mandarins, Elaine loves them. They're guardians in the full sense, having stepped in when her parents divorced. They are also old enough to remember when the family was less wealthy, and so see themselves as husbanders of resources. Leeming tells them they need to take out $8,000,000 for the ransom, that the insurance will only pay the "return indemnification" a postiori.

"It's an enormous sum," says the aunt. "Unspeakable!"

"Normally it would be complicated to unblock immediately," says the uncle. "We realize these are not normal times."

"But I don't want you to unblock it immediately," says Leeming.

The aunt and uncle stare. Even Coughlin stares. They've spoken about stalling the kidnappers to show they are on top of the situation. Acting too fast to satisfy demands often has tragic results—it indicates panic on the part of the families. Throwing the kidnappers off-balance will make them work to stay on-balance. A hard position to take after the last incident, yet Leeming's expression is cool. He remembers Elaine's way of saying "Interesting times we're living in," at any untoward situation. He'd answer "Too interesting for me," but she managed to inculcate a cheerfully stoic spirit in the both of them.

"How long are you going to wait?" asks the aunt, gripping her husband's hand.

"Six days," says Coughlin.

"Eight days," corrects Leeming.

"Unspeakable," says the aunt.

A million dollars is banal nowadays. An upper-middle-class person's mortgage. Mid-career balance of a 401(k). Ballplayer's salary—average ballplayer. Figures Leeming plays with on the computer every day—amortization, write-down, tax credit. But one million US in front of him, neatly stacked, bound with paper wrapping, is something else. It brings back the magic of One Million Dollars.

"Only the first installment," says Coughlin. "The rest is in transit, you might say."

"You could do a lot with all this," he says to Coughlin.

"The kidnappers could do a lot with it. They've probably

already made a list."

Leeming riffles one of the packets, the sound relatively soft. Hardly crisp new bills.

"Serial numbers all mixed up, like they wanted," says Coughlin. "Untraceable. Don't worry, they won't be holding it very long."

The plan calls for the cash to be put into the hands of Coughlin's operatives, proceeding according to the itinerary worked out with the kidnappers. Elaine will be deposited on a remote ridge as soon as the delivery is confirmed by the bagmen. Bayonese security forces will be stationed nearby, but only to whisk her away, not to intervene. As for US authorities, there's to be some role regarding surveillance, so far rather vague.

Leeming blanches at the realization that in this effort to save his wife they are treating her like a commodity. He walks over to the window as the cash is carefully packed into the valise. Leeming gazes down at the automobile lights flickering through the smog and the colored neon starting to flash on. The valise looks like something you travel with, an over-night bag, and when Leeming grabs it from the startled flunky it's like taking a bag from a porter at the airport.

"This much money, we should handle it ourselves," he says in Coughlin's direction.

"We?" says Coughlin.

"Me and you." Leeming lets his mouth form a half-smile, while keeping a grip on the handle of the valise. "You and me."

Coughlin agrees, does not balk, recognizing the client's imperative. But he gives Leeming a cockeyed look that he tries to suppress but can't.

*

The road follows a ravine but you can't see it through the verdure. Green and hazy, the landscape creates itself every hundred yards or so. The car is a late-model Baruda imported from India.

"You'd think they were developed enough to import from Korea at least," says Coughlin. "Rust bucket. Anyway we ain't got a long ways to go."

Coughlin drives, Leeming rides shotgun, the valise sits in the backseat. They are to go as far as the rendezvous, hand over the money to the operatives, and wait for things to reach their resolution. Overhead is the sound of light aircraft.

"They're going to raise altitude," says Coughlin. "So as not to give anyone ideas. They can survey just as well with high-powered sights."

"Can they see us?" says Leeming.

"They're not looking for us."

"No."

No reason they should. The lens above will be fixed on the rendezvous and what happens afterwards. Likewise, the kidnappers will be watching the route from wherever they are. He and Coughlin are outside everyone's field of vision. This is the culmination, thinks Leeming. In a strange way, he doesn't want it to end. Not like this. Treating her like a commodity, and him like a mere go-between.

"I don't trust them," he says.

"What? Trust who?"

"None of them. Not even the operatives. We don't need to give them the cash."

"You're nuts," says Coughlin. "It's all been worked out!"

Beginning to sweat, Coughlin looks intently at Leeming.

"I didn't mean it like that. But you got to get a grip on yourself, Mr. Leeming. My plan is all worked out. I mean our plan."

Leeming has no plan, only a dreamlike vision of how things are going to go.

"I don't trust you, either," says Leeming. "I want you to stop. Immediately."

"I ain't stopping," says Coughlin, turning dark, boiling red.

"I'm your employer. I'm paying you."

Coughlin's eyes flick here and there, up and down, like ricocheting pebbles, most frequently on the valise.

"Last time I checked, my retainer wasn't coming from your bank account."

"Then just stop and let me out!" Leeming shouts.

"Fuck no!" Coughlin's fingers on the wheel, tense like metal cables.

In the end, Leeming doesn't have to do anything. When the bend appears, Coughlin's hands are so rigid they can't turn the wheel in time. It's like a dream of flying. First the car sails like

Chitty Chitty Bang Bang over the guard rail. Then, from the bottom of the ravine where he lies, Leeming sees the valise fly as well, into a spot he etches into memory, even as he begins to lose consciousness. As his thoughts drift and vision hazes over, he sees Elaine on the ridge, waiting with two kidnappers. Suddenly, she pushes one, then the other, and both go flying over. Scrambling down the hillside, oddly-dressed in men's clothes, she meets the forces of law and order. It's a dream with a happy end.

*

Leeming wakes up in pain, and in a state of surprise. He expects to be taken to a hospital, or at least a field clinic. In his sleep, or half-sleep, he felt his body being moved, and this became yet another dream, of transport by helicopter. He sees now that he is in some sort of shantytown shack. The room is sizeable, with crates scattered about, so he assumes he's in a shop's stockroom. They must have stopped at the nearest establishment. Perhaps he was too badly injured to be moved. This produces momentary panic, until he senses his condition isn't quite that grave. It's possible that Coughlin is in worse condition, and he anxiously tries to reconstruct events, to assure himself that it wasn't his fault.

Tambol and a few officers come in the room. He doesn't say anything to Leeming, not even to his men. Looking down at Leeming momentarily, but with intensity, he goes to the four corners of the room, checking them like a building inspector.

"You must rest," says Tambol, talking to the wall. "Big bump on the road. Bad roads here, no money for roads."

"What about Mr. Coughlin?" says Leeming, sitting up. It's as if he feels more responsible for the kidnap consultant than for his wife. Coughlin had committed to the safety of his family, even if it was for a fee, plus expenses.

"Don't worry about him." Tambol says it with finality, pursing his lips firmly then spitting a bullet of saliva onto the floor. "We'll be back later to brief."

They all leave, except for one officer, who silently changes a dressing on Leeming's upper arm. He hadn't been aware of it, but now realizes he's numb there. The man, young and thin, looks more like a male nurse than a police officer, but before he leaves he puts a shackle on Leeming's ankle, and attaches it to the foot of the cot.

"They think I'm a criminal?" says Leeming, more to himself than the young man, who in any case doesn't reply. The man silently leaves the room, and locks the door.

*

"You like making videos, mister? Video camera, cheap, cheap!" Tambol is making his jokes again.

Leeming is taken out of the room, and brought to the adjoining one. A camera on a tripod faces a wall, bare except for a table and chair in front of it. The wall is pitted cement, like the ravaged skin of the more unfortunate locals. A few of the policemen, even Tambol, also have less than comely complexions. They make him sit on the chair, like someone posing for a high school graduation photo. He folds his hands and rests them on the table, but they begin to tremble. Leeming exerts pressure on his enlaced fingers and thinks of the bag of cash in the forest.

"You read this," says Tambol, more gravely now, as he unfolds a piece of paper. "A message that you are okay. But not okay completely."

If that was a joke, he didn't laugh at it. After giving Leeming the paper, Tambol casually slips a ski mask over his face. The other police officers do the same. They all position themselves behind Leeming, in formation, as if this is part of the graduation photo shoot, a group portrait. Leeming thinks harder about the money, doing his best not to let his bowels give out.

"I am being held for ransom of $500,000. I have not been harmed. The kidnappers are civilized people, they just want money. Please, to avoid any problems, pay the ransom within one week according to instructions which will follow shortly. I love you all."

Leeming can't help smiling. Curiously, his fear has left him. He feels gratitude to Tambol. The man's clarity is like one of those curvy, locally-made knives, opening up many possibilities. Leeming knows where $1,000,000 is. He can offer to split it with them. Or he can wait to see if his side will cough up, or negotiate. Anyway, one week is plenty of time in which to see if escape is possible. You never know what tomorrow will bring during the interesting times we live in.

From the UV Files

File #33
RILEY SPILMAN

45 29

Cat heads float around this city
Like Cheshires with grey whiskers
Moving in riddles found on newspaper stands
Saying something about the murders
People bring their televisions outside
And watch it in the garden SOME SPECTACLE

They fear the storm cloud moving in
With all the ravages of history
That might bury them all
Only when one wanders alone in this place
They remember
Someone is cutting the heads off cats

Follow the trail of red memories
Search for it
Search for the [window]
And the entire world will come together
All of it now:

The first was a twenty something
Prostitute dumped on the outskirts of the city
Investigation was clumsy
A semen sample lost
Murder ignored until added
With the others

The body of a girl, nineteen
About two miles from the city
Hair matted with blood
Although no visible cuts on the head
Face swollen from blunt trauma
Marks on the neck suggest strangulation
Both legs were recently broken

From the UV Files

Anal and vaginal tearing
Not clear on cause of death
Her eyes watch the West

A day later an old man came across another corpse
On his way home from the factory
The body was impaled with a metal rod
Arms spread out like Christ
Extensive damage to the face
She was gagged with a rag
Blood was found under her nails
A stab wound in the abdomen
(That seemed to have occurred after death)
Possibly fourteen years of age
No one has claimed her body

Another
Found twenty meters from the last
Crude cuts on the body
Signs of rape and struggle
Both eyes missing
Either a bird or the killers responsible
Nearby the prints of possibly four horses

Tomorrow once again
Black hair blue eyes
Early twenties
Half buried in the desert
Her right breast torn away
As if chewed off
Skirt in tatters cut up like her body
Decomposition will place the murder
Six to eight days old
No one will claim her

Despite numerous suspects and arrests
The list of victims grows at a steady pace
The tally shows
45 girls

From the UV Files

29 cats

So we forget these things
And return to our corners

Between the alleys and the cafes
Lies an emptiness that flows
With the skeletons of Mexican girls
Mixing with all those bones
Deep in the sand and aquifers
And between those the seals that separate and bind
Seem and seeming
Jazz horns paint the horizon
In colors of mosquitos
Seven sound in unison

The city cannot hold
It is born

You go home in a brown haze
As the rust cloud descends on the city
Washing away the cigarette butts and bodies and dreams
You search around your house only to find
Nothing
In the cupboards, empty cups
Shredded paper topples over a desk
A flutter of wings and a distant moan
The cats flee and whisper its name
As they fade into the carnivorous mouths of factories
To escape the cloud descending like a nude

The [window] turns an iceberg at night
And outside becomes a cold enigma

You follow a noise but the building creaks with old cats
And your last cup of coffee is empty
Not there
Looking inside the hollow
You think not all is empty in there

From the UV Files

Then you turn and waiting outside the [window]
You see it

From the UV Files

File# 37
DANIEL DAVIS

To Good Ends

I heard the boys shouting for me, so I ran to the open door of the house and onto the porch. Luke and Manley were propping a third individual between them, and it took me a moment to recognize him. I took in his torn clothes and the blood and dirt smeared all over him, then I said, "Boys, bring him in."

They carried the man in and laid him on the sofa. He was groaning, his eyes closed but conscious. When the boys had him down I said, "Take the truck around back. Then clean yourselves up and come right back here."

I could tell they weren't too eager to leave, but I looked hard at them and Manley took the hint. He grabbed his brother and they went outside. I listened to them on the porch, watching the man. Helen was standing in the kitchen, staring at me, but instead of asking what was going on she said, "Hot or cold water?"

"Cold," I said. "Oren's a mite thirsty, I reckon."

He opened his eyes and squinted at me. "I know you, mister?"

"Hobbes." I dragged a chair next to the couch and sat down. "Jeb Hobbes."

"Oh." He half-smiled at me, then looked away. "Didn't recognize you."

"It's been a while. Didn't know you were still around."

"I wasn't."

"Where you working now?"

"The Peterson place. Their eldest boy joined the army, so they've been needing an extra hand."

Helen brought the water in, and she saw who was on the couch and said, "Well, Oren Kendall. What brings you back here in such fine condition?"

He sat up a little, wincing, and took the glass she handed him. "Money, Mrs. Hobbes. Gotta say it's money, like always."

"Indeed." When he was done drinking she took the glass and asked if he wanted another. He didn't, and looked at me, and I nodded to Helen. She went into the kitchen and didn't reappear.

We sat in silence for a few minutes, him gently lifting his leg. I glanced at the one he'd been favoring, his left, and saw that the ankle seemed a little swollen.

"Might have to cut the boot off," I said.

He nodded, and we just sat there again until the boys came back in. They came immediately over to the couch, and I told Luke, "Close the door."

"But it's hotter 'n hell in here."

"Close the door."

He did, and when he was done I told the boys to head upstairs. They groaned a bit, but I think Manley might've had an idea what I meant, 'cause he hauled his brother away. When they were gone, I eyed the kitchen, where Helen had disappeared, and I said, "All right, Oren. We're alone. What you doing on my land?"

"Runnin'," he said. He pointed at his leg. "That damn cattle guard ya'll put in. Must be new."

"Two years ago. Can't say as it's been worth the price."

"Yeah, well. It works, Mr. Hobbes, it works."

"What you runnin' from, son?"

He shrugged and sat himself straighter. It must've hurt, but Kendall was always one to look you in the eye when he spoke, and he needed to be level with me.

"A man runs bad enough to twist his ankle," I said, "he must know what it is he's runnin' from."

"Maybe it's best you don't know, Mr. Hobbes."

I nodded. "Damn right it's best I don't know. But fact of the matter is, son, I'm gonna know, ain't I?"

"I reckon so, sir."

"So." I waited. He said nothing, didn't even look at me—he was looking out the window, and I soon followed his gaze. It was flat out there, flat and barren, the fields dusty and ill-used. The weather had been bad this summer, real bad, and the cattle weren't eating well enough, and the beans didn't appear to be coming in right. It could all turn around, I knew, but I'd seen enough summers like this to know we'd have to skimp this winter. And even then, the odds weren't good.

I was the first to give in. I could've waited, could've been sympathetic; after all, he'd always been nice to my boys, always respected my wife and I. But I had to remain objective; out here, that's the only way to do things, sometimes.

"How they travelin', Oren? They got a truck or horses?"

"Horses," he said. "They're horseback."

I nodded. That would slow them down a bit more, make it just that much harder to track. Though, aside from the Peterson ranch, there wasn't another property this side of town for miles. Assuming Kendall would be heading into town—as they surely would—he would almost certainly have to cross my property. Bad luck he hadn't known about the cattle guard, and bad luck he'd been too panicked to look for it.

"How many?"

"Three. Brothers, I think. Two of 'em look alike."

"You owe them money, Oren?"

"No."

No further explanation. He was still staring out the window, his ankle forgotten. I watched his hand groping at his jeans, the fingers clenching unconsciously. I wondered what he was trying to clutch, in his tangled mind; what was he grasping at, what was he attacking? He must've felt my eyes, because when I looked up from his hand he was looking at me.

"I'm sorry, Mr. Hobbes," he said. "I'm truly sorry 'bout this."

It didn't much matter whether he was sorry or not, I told him; it was happening, that was all there was to it. Nobody's fault, not his or mine or even God's, probably. If anything, best to blame the three men coming for him, best to blame the motivations of such men.

That's what I told him. Inside, I was cursing him, wishing him to get the hell out of my house and go as far as his bum leg would take him. That ain't the kind of thing you say to a man in need, but it's often the kind of thing you think. I guess he must've seen it in my eyes 'cause he said, "I can go out the back, Mr. Hobbes. Just go and keep goin'. Maybe I can hide out there somewhere."

"Nowhere to hide," I said, which wasn't saying I didn't wish there was. "Flat as hell out there, son."

"Yes, sir."

I saw something move from the corner of my eye. Helen was there in the kitchen, and I knew she'd been listening. I said to

Kendall, "I'll get you another glass of water," and I got up and joined her.

She probably had about as much fear in her eyes as I did in mine. She said, "Jeb. The boys."

"I know." I listened for them upstairs. I wondered if they'd been listening in as well.

Helen was whispering, her voice a bare rasp against the heat. "We have to get him out of here."

"We can't." I went past her and got a glass of water. As I was passing her again I leaned in close and said, "You know I would," although I'm not sure if she knew any such thing.

I went back and gave Kendall the glass. He took a small sip from it then set it on the table beside the couch. He nodded towards the window. "They're comin', Mr. Hobbes."

I looked. I could see the dust first, then the vague shapes of three men on horseback. I counted off in my head how many men in the county still went on horseback, but there was quite a big number, so I said, "Who are they, Oren?"

He didn't answer.

"The law?"

"No."

We watched the men draw closer. It took a long time before I could see them clearly enough to identify them: three men and four horses. Two of the men did look alike, and the third was a little older, and he carried himself like the colonels I'd seen in the war. He was also dressed better than the other two, in the same shabby clothes but with more care as to presentation. I could see the sun reflecting off his buttons before I could even see his face.

I knew the three by sight but not by name; I pegged them as from Shelby County, maybe Handover. Not necessarily local boys, but I'd seen them in town from time to time, which meant I'd probably seen them at the Sheriff's Office when I went to vote or pay bills. I wasn't sure if that was a good thing or not. They weren't law; I would've recognized them if they were law. Except the man in front. He'd been law at one point, 'cause he was too young to have been in the war, and yet he certainly wasn't no regular hillbilly.

Kendall and I watched them until they rode up and stopped a few feet from the porch. The boys must've been looking too, because they came to the edge of the stairs and Manley said, "Pa?"

"Go upstairs," I told him. "Shut yourselves in your room."

They did. Helen was standing at the entrance to the kitchen again. I asked her, "Anyone around back?"

"No."

"Good." I stood up and went to the door. I glanced out the window again first, and the well-dressed one saw me and dismounted his horse. I opened the door and stepped out, leaving it open behind me.

The man stood a few feet from the base of my porch, looking up at me. He was in his late twenties, with a groomed mustache and gelled hair beneath his hat. His eyes were pale blue, and in them I could see a gentleness that I didn't believe for a second. The tautness of his shoulders, his hands held just off his holsters said otherwise.

The two men on the horses were definitely brothers, in their late teens or early twenties, with unkempt beards and hats that had seen more sun than was customary. One of the men had a revolver half-drawn; the other held a rifle at his side, aimed down and forward.

"Good afternoon," the well-dressed one said.

I nodded at him. "Good afternoon."

Silence. I met his eyes and held them, but it wasn't easy. He smiled a little and said, "Allow me to introduce myself. Jeremiah McClellan."

I didn't say anything, just looked up at his companions.

"William and Everett," McClellan said. "Friends of mine."

"Jeb Hobbes," I said. Neither of us offered to shake hands.

"Mr. Hobbes."

I stood within just a foot of the door. He was eyeing the house, paying special attention to the windows. The two on horseback were just looking at me, and I was doing my best to ignore them.

"Mr. Hobbes," McClellan said again. He seemed not to like my name much. "I believe we got us a situation, do we not?"

"I reckon we do. You're on my property."

"We are." He nodded somberly. "And without your kind permission, I regret. No time for formalities. The nature of our business requires us to proceed with promptness and haste, which lends itself, by its very nature, to rudeness. My apologies."

I shrugged.

"But Mr. Hobbes, it is our business which brings us here." He nodded at the door behind me. "You've a man in there, I presume."

"I may have."

McClellan smiled at me, then called out, "Oren Kendall!"

Kendall didn't respond. McClellan watched me the whole time. After a few seconds of silence he said, "Is he conscious?"

When I didn't say anything he continued, "Mr. Hobbes, it would be best if you answered my questions with all due haste and veracity."

"Yes."

"Can he walk?"

"Depends."

"Depends on what he's walking to, or depends on how he's walking?"

"Both."

McClellan licked his lips. He glanced up at one of the upper story windows, and I was tempted to follow his gaze but I kept my eyes on his face. He looked back at me, smiling again, but it wasn't quite as comfortable this time, which meant it was more genuine and I relaxed slightly. The way you relax when the wolf has finally revealed itself in full—you know where it is, you know that it's not at your back.

"What is he to you, Mr. Hobbes? Besides a man who stumbled in here injured and hurried."

"It don't matter." I eyed the revolver at his waist, then the guns of the two brothers. "He's here with me, and not with you."

"I assure you, if you knew what he'd done, you'd let me walk in there and retrieve him."

"Would I?"

McClellan laughed a little. "Mr. Hobbes. You aren't a man for this. Let me get him."

"No."

"Then bring him out here."

"Can't."

"Won't, you mean."

"All right."

"If I told you I was well within my rights to go in there

anyways and get him."

"I'd call you a liar, Mr. McClellan. I don't see any badges."

"A badge is a piece of metal, Mr. Hobbes. Any man can carry one."

"Then you get yourselves some and come back."

I could see the two horseback men getting restless. The man with the pistol had it drawn in full now; it was resting across his lap, but I figured he could have it up and firing at my chest in less than a second. The other had lifted the barrel of his rifle, so that it was now aimed in my general direction. McClellan hadn't drawn his revolver any further, but he hadn't moved his hand away from it either.

"You gonna shoot an unarmed man?" I asked. "An unarmed man who ain't done nothin' wrong?"

"You're harboring a fugitive," McClellan said. "That counts as wrong in most books."

"A fugitive from what? The law?"

"From justice."

I nodded. "Well then. Sheriff Haney handles the justice around these parts. You bring him out here, we'll talk."

McClellan leaned forward. He took a couple steps, until he was almost on the porch. "Mr. Hobbes. We got no need of the sheriff in this. This is a personal matter, to be settled by me and the boys here. While I've no doubt the law would side with us, we have no time for decisions to be made. Even your decision is, I dare say, an inconvenience."

"Too bad. I've decided."

"Would you like to know why we want him?"

"No."

"Maybe you'd like to ride out to the Peterson ranch. Maybe you'd like to see what's happened to Valerie Peterson. Her husband. Her kids."

I said nothing. I glanced out at the fields, in the general direction of the Peterson ranch, and I watched my cattle grazing. They were thin, almost too thin; I hadn't the money for good feed any more, and I could see this farm slipping away from me like water from a leaky faucet. My boys wouldn't be farmers; Manley was good at it but also good at school, and Luke just didn't have the interest. I didn't blame them—the boys they went to school with weren't from farming families, most of them. Their fathers worked at the mill; a few worked at the bank, or the groceries. My boys didn't know many farmers' sons, and I can't say I was all that upset by it. Good kids will come to good ends; that's what my father told me, and it worked out well enough in my favor, more or less.

"Don't think of him as a man," McClellan said. "Think of him as an animal. A coyote in your barn that you need to get rid of. A creature that will cause harm to your family if he remains inside your home."

McClellan's horse was getting restless. It stamped a little, and he turned and whistled at it. The horse walked up to him and nuzzled his throat. He pet its muzzle and turned back to me. "We are leaving here with him, Mr. Hobbes. You know this."

"Do I?"

"You aren't a man for this. I've seen you before, your kind. You're a good man, Mr. Hobbes, but you're not one for this precisely because you're a good man. Myself and the boys here, we're good men too, but we're a different sort of good, the kind that sees its share of blood every now and then. The kind that doesn't need badges, Mr. Hobbes, because if we had badges, we wouldn't be any different than we are now. You understand me?"

The brothers were watching the house now, the upper windows. Taking stock of who all might be watching. One of them even got the idea that there might be someone else around, and craned his neck about. We were far from the road, and no other homes were in sight. I liked the isolation, and so did Helen, but just at that moment I wished we lived in the heart of town, right next to the bank and the Sheriff's Office. Haney wasn't the most sober or competent man I knew of, but I also knew worse, and I was certain he could handle a gun far better than I could.

"Mr. Hobbes, I need to be sure you're listening to me."

I turned my eyes from the brothers back to McClellan. "I'm listening."

"And are you hearing me?"

"I am."

"Oren Kendall, despite what you may think, despite whatever state he may be in, is not a good man. Because I know you have family listening, I won't go into the particulars of his crimes. But rest assured, Mr. Hobbes, if you had been out at the

Peterson ranch, you would hand him over to me with a ribbon around his neck."

"I want you off my property," I said. "Or I'll call for Sheriff Haney."

McClellan was smiling now. He knew it was pretense and nothing else. "You do that, Mr. Hobbes. And maybe, by the time he gets here, there'll still be a house standing." He nodded towards the horses. "Picked up some kerosene from the Peterson ranch. We can have us a little fire right here, no fuss, no trouble."

I figured he was bluffing—I didn't see any kerosene—but I saw the opportunity not to call him on it and took it. I swallowed, my throat dry and sticky, and nodded. I stepped back into the house, where it wasn't any cooler, and turned to Kendall on the sofa.

He was watching me. The dust on his cheeks was running with his tears, and he said, "Mr. Hobbes—"

I stopped him. "I'm sorry, Oren. I have my boys."

Helen looked at me, and even though she was nodding, I couldn't lift my head to her. To Kendall, I said, "Please, Oren. I don't want that man in my home."

He didn't argue further. He let me get my shoulder under him for support, and I led him to our door. His tears had stopped, but he mumbled, "I didn't mean no harm by it." I didn't respond because he wasn't talking to me.

McClellan had ascended the porch steps. He took Kendall's other shoulder, glancing down at Kendall's left foot. "Hello, Oren. Had an accident, I see."

Kendall didn't say anything, and McClellan led him to the spare horse. Kendall's bad ankle banged against a step once, and I thought for a moment that he was going to lose his composure, but all that slipped out was one loud sob, and then he clammed up. One of the brothers hopped down from his horse and helped McClellan put Kendall on the unaccompanied horse. Then the brother remounted, and McClellan turned to me.

"I appreciate your holding him for us, Mr. Hobbes. Very Christian of you. I wish you and your family the very best."

He got on his horse, and the four of them rode off, Kendall's horse lagging behind, a rope stretched almost taut between them. Kendall looked back briefly, and when he did I turned away and went back into the house. The door stayed open behind me.

Helen was there waiting for me, and she hugged me. Luke and Manley came downstairs in a rush, and Luke said, "Pa, why'd we give him up?"

"Yeah," Manley said, though I'd almost expected more of him. "We have guns. We could've fought them off. Oren would've done the same for us."

Kendall wouldn't have, and I almost told them that, but Helen said, "Boys, I think we can use a good meal after all this. Why don't you help me with the preparations? Your father needs a few minutes to himself."

The three of them went into the kitchen, the boys still saying I should've fought the men off. And listening to them, part of me agreed. It was a small part, an irrational part, and it said there had only been three of the men, and all four of us in the house—plus Kendall himself—knew how to shoot. We could've fought them, before they burned down the house, and held them off until Haney and his deputy got there. It would've been bloody, but we could've done it, and Kendall would still be on the sofa where I sat.

But he wasn't there, he was gone, and I had the other part of me—the part that McClellan had seen, the part he'd mocked, in his own way—to thank for it. I also had my wife, and my boys.

I decided, in the morning, to take out the damn cattle guard. It was more trouble than it was worth. I'd be able to trade the metal for feed, and put a little more meat on those cows. And maybe, come next year, there'd still be something left of the farm I'd managed to protect.

From the UV Files

File# 47
STEVEN GULVEZAN

For the love of Oona

High noon at Kroger
A 60-year-old

Grosse Pointe Woods man
Was arrested for shoplifting

In excess of one hundred dollars
Assault and battery

And attempting to flee
The scene of a crime.

Police said the suspect
Loaded up a shopping cart

With four 12-packs of Guinness Draught beer
Valued at $58.78

Angus steaks
Valued at $99.18

Multiple packages of jumbo shrimp
Valued at $103.89

Four bottles of Cook's Grand Reserve champagne
Valued at $28.98

Multiple cases of Red Bull
Valued at $103.99

A box of Trojan condoms
Valued at $18.39

And a pack of Zestra Feminine Arousal Fluid

From the UV Files

Valued at $25.99

When the suspect exited without paying
A Kroger loss prevention officer
Confronted him

The suspect
Pushed the cart into the officer
Knocked over flower shelves

And pushed other shopping carts
In the officer's direction

As he attempted to flee
Police cruisers

Responding to the call
Cut off the suspect's escape

In the parking lot of Kroger
The suspect was tackled

By four responding policemen
And after a brief struggle

Was tasered
And taken into custody

As he was dragged
To the rear of a police cruiser

The suspect was heard
To cry out

Something
About doing it all

For the love of Oona
And that was all

From the UV Files

He was able to say
Before the officers

Tasered him
Just once more

To make sure
He was amenable to his fate

From the UV Files

File #50
WILLIAM J. FEDIGAN

Love Kills Slow

Dominic "Lover Boy" Romeo, hand in pocket, squeezing his hairy balls tight the way he does when he gets twitchy—talking to Jimmy low so nobody hears. Jimmy listening hard with both ears, staring into his coffee, turning cold as ice.

"It's gotta be today. *Today!*" Dominic whispering loud, poking the table top when he says it. Jimmy's coffee cup jumps. Jimmy jumps. Jimmy's scared. Jimmy's scared shitless. *Jimmy's buttfucked big time...*

Jimmy owes Dominic large—and Jimmy's short. Jimmy knows if you owe, you die slow.

Dominic's saying to Jimmy, "You do this thing for me today, we're even. Every fuckin penny. *Even.*"

"Even?"

"Every fuckin penny. But you don't do this thing today, you gotta a big fuckin problem. *Understand?*"

"But I never hurt nobody before, Mr. Romeo... Not like the way you want me to."

"You hurt me, you piece of shit! When you owe me and you don't pay, you hurt me. When you hurt me, I gotta hurt you. Understand?"

"But I don't know if I can do this thing to a woman, Mr. Romeo... Maybe there's something else I can do..."

"Let's make this fuckin simple: *I own you, asshole!* You breathe because I say you breathe. I don't want you to breathe, you stop breathing. *Understand?* You're like...like a fuckin rat in a trap. My fuckin rat in my fuckin trap! *Understand?*"

"Yeah, yeah, Mr. Romeo. I understand," Jimmy says, smelling cheese, feeling his neck about to be snapped.

"Use this. I took it off a little faggot owed me large," Dominic says, sliding the little faggot's gun under the table to Jimmy. "Hides in you pocket, real nice. Light as a fuckin feather. Take it. *Take it!*"

Jimmy takes the little faggot's gun, light as a fuckin feather... but it's heavy as lead in Jimmy's hand. Jimmy's doesn't feel good holding it in his hand. Jimmy feels sick holding it in his hand. Jimmy wants to run. Jimmy wants to drop the little faggot's gun and run, but he knows he can't. *Jimmy's rat-trapped big time...*

Dominic's twitchy now, squeezing his hairy balls tight, saying to Jimmy, "I gotta know now, can you do this thing for me? *Now!* Understand?"

"Ok ok. I do this thing today, you and me are even. Right?"

"How many fuckin times I gotta tell you. You do this thing for me today, we're even. Every fuckin penny. *Even.*"

"Suppose something happens, it gets fucked-up," Jimmy says, holding his breath.

"It gets fucked up, then you and me, we're un-even," Dominic says, flipping the table over onto Jimmy's lap, coffee spilling on Jimmy, coffee cup hitting the dirty floor, breaking in a million fuckin pieces. "*Understand!*"

Jimmy looking at the million fuckin pieces, looking at the dirty floor, insides turning to pus, says, "Ok ok, Mr. Romeo. Take it easy. I understand."

"I figured you would. Now, like I been sayin, it's gotta be today. *Today!* Understand?" Dominic's hairy balls hurting like a son of a bitch.

"Ok ok. I'll do it today. Tell me again, Mr. Romeo. Tell me again about her. What she looks like. You said she's a heavy woman."

"Heavy? She's a fat fuckin pig. She's the Goodyear fuckin blimp. Couldn't hide her in a freak show, for chrissakes."

"Ok, ok. And she goes to the park every day."

"Every fuckin day, rain or shine, she's in the park feeding the fuckin pigeons stale bagels. Every fuckin day, same thing."

"And you said she's gotta big tat on her arm."

"Yeah. In case you miss her—which would be fuckin impossible—she's got a big tat on her arm says, LOVE KILLS SLOW."

"What kind of woman has a tat says, LOVE KILLS SLOW?"

"A fat fuck feeds pigeons stale bagels. Who the fuck knows, for chrissakes," Romeo says, twitchy and squeezing hard.

"Ok ok, Mr. Romeo."

"Now shut the fuck up and listen. I'm gonna tell you how

you're gonna do it."

"Ok ok, Mr. Romeo," Jimmy says, teeth grinding, stomach tight, listening hard with both ears.

"You're gonna go to the park today and sit next to her. Throw some stale bagels at the fuckin pigeons, make conversation, whatever. After couple minutes of bullshittin, you say to her real sweet, *Mr. Romeo sends his love to Juliet on this special day...*"

"Her name's *Juliet*, Mr. Romeo?" Jimmy says, thinking maybe he heard it wrong, maybe it's a joke—*Romeo and Juliet?*...Maybe...

"You gotta problem with her fuckin name, for chrissakes?!" Dominic about to pull both hairy balls outta their socket.

"No no. No problem, Mr. Romeo. Sorry, Mr. Romeo," Jimmy says, thinking, *Jesus fucking Christ...Romeo and Juliet...*

"Now tell me what you're gonna say, and it's gotta be perfect. *Understand?*

"Ok ok, Mr. Romeo. I'm gonna say, *Mr. Romeo sends his love to Juliet on this special day*. I'm gonna say it real sweet."

"Yeah. You say it real sweet—then shoot her two times in the face with the little faggot's gun. Not in the belly. With all that fat who the fuck knows where the slugs'll end up. *Understand?*

"In the face only. Two times in the face only," Jimmy says; stomach flip-flops like a fish with a hook in its eye.

"Just two more fuckin things."

"What's that, Mr. Romeo?"

"Number one, you fuck it up, I'll blow your balls to shit. Number two, change your fuckin pants. Looks like you pissed yourself, for chissakes. *Understand?*

Jimmy looking at his pants, coffee soaking his crotch, turning cold as ice.

Dominic watching Jimmy close, knowing Jimmy's trying to figure a way out of this thing...but Dominic's got Jimmy by the hairy balls—and *he's squeezing tight.*

*

Jimmy wearing clean pants now, in the park now, watching Juliet, fat-fuck ugly, sitting on a bench, slats under her ass about to break, feeding pigeons stale bagels.

Jimmy fingering the little faggot's gun in his pocket,

fingering the garlic bagel in his pocket, feeling sick, going over and over it in his head: *Mr.Romeo sends his love to...to...two times in the face...in the face only...*

Jimmy's shaky, wondering if he can do this thing, crushing the stale bagel in his pocket, moving towards her...

Jimmy sitting on the bench now, looking at her, big as the Goodyear fuckin blimp he's gotta pop pop...two times in the face...

Jimmy looking at her tat: big heart, knife sticking thru it, blood dripping down, says LOVE KILLS SLOW under the heart, capital letters.

Jimmy's looking close, thinking, *Jesus fucking Christ.*

"What you lookin at?" Juliet says.

"Nuthin," Jimmy says.

"I saw you lookin at my tat."

"Oh yeah. I was. Nice tat."

"Can't you read asshole? Says: LOVE KILLS SLOW. Nice tat?"

Jimmy looking at her when she says it, her eyes gray as nails, pounding holes into his head.

"Sorry," Jimmy says, looking away, not knowing what the fuck to do next...

"*Stick to the plan*," he thinks. "*Feed the pigeons first...then Mr. Romeo sends his love to...to...two times in the face...*"

Jimmy reaches in his pocket for the bagel...*feed the pigeons first*... and the little faggot's gun falls out. The little faggot's gun smells like garlic... and... lilac powder and sweat. Jimmy gags. Jimmy can't breathe.

Juliet's got Jimmy in a headlock. Jimmy's suffocating in her armpit.

"Who the fuck sent you," she says, squeezing Jimmy blind.

"Mis-ster...Row...Me...Oh...," Jimmy choking out the words.

"Lover Boy sent you? I knew somebody would be comin for me today, but not a stupid motherfucker like you—with a squirt gun couldn't kill a fuckin fly."

Juliet's holding the little faggot's gun now, laughing loud, fat jiggling hard. Jimmy's seeing stars, smelling garlic, lilacs and sweat.

She lets go of Jimmy. He falls down. She puts her foot on

his chest. Jimmy can't move.

"Why did Lover Boy send you of all fuckin people?"

"I owe Mr. Romeo large, and he said I shoot you, him and me, we're even, every fuckin penny, even. It's what he said."

"It's *me* Lover Boy owes large! *Should be me shooting him, for chrissakes.*"

"I don't nothing about that. I don't know shit."

"Then I'll tell you about it—*then I'll tell you what you're gonna do about it*," she says, foot on Jimmy's chest, crushing his heart. Jimmy trying to breathe, thinking, *Jesus fucking Christ.*

"To make a long fuckin story short, on this day, on this bench, ten years ago, me and Lover Boy meet. He's feedin the pigeons like me. We start talking. He tells me he likes big women. He tells me I'm beautiful. He tells me a lot of shit. One thing leads to another, we get married. The marriage is good until it gets bad…real bad, real fuckin bad…It's so bad he won't touch me anymore. Do you know what that feels like, being a woman like me, not being touched anymore? It's like having cancer. It's like dying slow," she says.

"THE MOTHERFUCKER BROKE MY HEART!" Her voice cracks like ice when she says it, like glass when she says it…

"Wait a minute, wait a minute," Jimmy says, catching his breath, putting the pieces together. "You and Mr. Romeo are married? You're *Juliet Romeo*?"

"You gotta fuckin problem with my name, asshole?" She's frozen over and frosted again…

"No, no problem…Except Mr. Romeo wants you dead."

"I won't divorce him is why."

"But he wants you dead, you don't divorce him."

"I tell him it's because we're fuckin Catholics. I tell him ask the fuckin Pope, for chrissakes. But the truth is I won't divorce him because I hate the motherfucker. HE BROKE MY FUCKIN HEART! Understand?"

"But he wants you dead!"

"You keep sayin that, asshole."

"But…"

"But nuthin. It ends today. *You're gonna end it…today.* And this is *how* you're gonna end it today," she says, pulling a gun, size of a cannon, color of a tombstone, outta her pocketbook.

From the UV Files

Jimmy's looking at the cannon, color of a tombstone, almost seeing his name carved in.

"*Take it!*" She hands the cannon to Jimmy. "You're gonna pay Lover Boy a visit today. You tell him you did it, that I'm dead in the park with the fuckin pigeons. Then you tell him my last words were *words of love*. You tell him I said: *Juliet sends her love to Mr. Romeo on this special day...*"

"But..but...That's what he said I should say to you..."

"I guess we're both fuckin romantics at heart. Now tell me what you're gonna say. It's gotta be perfect."

"I'm gonna say: *Juliet sends her love to Mr. Romeo on this special day*. I'm gonna say it real sweet."

"Yeah. Say it real sweet—then shoot him two times in the hand."

"In the hand?"

"In the hand."

"Which hand?"

"The hand that's in his pocket squeezin his hairy balls. You shoot him two times in the pocket with that cannon, the slugs'll go right his hand and blow his hairy balls to shit."

"Jesus fucking Christ, Mrs. Romeo. I don't know if I can..."

"Let's make this fuckin simple: *I own you, asshole*! You don't do it, it's your hairy balls blown to shit. You do it, you owe nobody nuthin. Not a fuckin penny. *Understand?*" She stares at Jimmy cold. Jimmy shakes and rattles.

"Ok..ok...I'll do it, Mrs. Romeo. Two times in the pocket, blow his hairy balls to shit. I'll do it today," Jimmy says, head spinning, rat-trapped again, *rat-trapped big time...*

"One more thing," she says, taking her foot offa Jimmy's chest. "After you shoot his hairy balls to shit, you wait. You watch and you wait until he stops breathin. He's gonna beg. He's gonna cry. He's gonna bleed all over your shoes. He's gonna flop around like a fish. He's gonna turn blue. He's gonna turn gray. You're gonna do nuthin but watch and wait. It's gonna take a long time, but you wait until he stops breathin...until the motherfucker stops breathin. *Understand?*"

"Jesus, Mrs. Romeo, you musta loved him a lot to hate him so much."

"What the fuck do you know about it, asshole?"

"Nuthin, Mrs. Romeo. Nuthin at all."

"That's right. You don't know nuthin about a woman's love—and you don't know shit about a woman's HATE!" She's spits all over Jimmy's face when she says it. The spit is hot like tears, like blood. The spit burns Jimmy's eyes.

"Ok ok, Mrs. Romeo. Take it easy," Jimmy says, spit-burned.

"Now tell me what you're gonna do before I blow *your* hairy balls to shit."

"I'm gonna watch and wait until he stops breathin,'" Jimmy says, trying to catch his breath.

"No matter how long it takes."

"No matter how long it takes, I wait," Jimmy says, turning blue, turning gray, trying to breathe.

"Like the sign says." Juliet's pointing to her tat, smiling. Jimmy reading it one more time: LOVE KILLS SLOW, capital letters.

*

Jimmy's walking away now, cannon in his pocket, still feeling her foot crushing his heart—like his heart was nothing at all—*like he was nothing at all.*

Jimmy all of a sudden feels crazy, dizzy crazy. He's thinking: LOVE KILLS SLOW... He's thinking: *Mr. Romeo sends his love...* He's thinking: *Juliet sends her love...* He's thinking: *Butt-fucked...* He's thinking: *Rat-trapped...* He's thinking: *I own you asshole...I own you...*

Jimmy's thinking he's gonna take the fucking cannon and blow Juliet's face off...blow Mr. Romeo's hairy balls to shit...

Jimmy holds the cannon in both hands, heart beating fast—too fast. Jimmy's thinking, re-thinking. He tries to stop thinking but can't stop thinking: *You do this, you'll be even, every fuckin penny... every fuckin penny...You don't do it, I'll blow your balls to shit...to shit...to shit...*

Jimmy's insides explode. Blood shoots from his heart to his hands to the cannon. He tries to throw it away, away from him, far away—*but he can't.*

He raises the cannon above his head and shoots it four times into a goddamned perfect blue sky—two times for Romeo's hairy balls, two for Juliet's fat fuckin face. Jimmy's smiling when he does it, when he shoots the cannon, when the bullets fly free—and up and away—far away…

People around Jimmy scream, run for cover. Jimmy's smiling wide.

He'll wait for the cops now, to grab him, throw him in a cell so he's safe for awhile—*for awhile.*

Jimmy drops the cannon. He feels cold—like ice. He shivers. He looks down. He's standing in pigeon shit. It looks like snow. It looks like fresh snow—clean, fresh snow. It reminds Jimmy of Christmas Day. Jimmy laughs, thinking, *"Christmas Day."*

Jimmy hears sirens, sees lights flashing like Christmas lights.

*

Jimmy's waiting for the cops now, thinking about Christmas Day, laughing, shivering, remembering it clear…remembering how Christmas Day was a good day, a great day—*the best day ever.*

File #58
PHILLIP GARDNER

The Future Never Lasts

Thin-faced Jenkins sat in the backseat of the Maxima, a black derby tilted to shield his eyes. He spoke into Penny's rearview mirror. "Is your last name really Cleavinger or did you just make that up on account of how you show off your stuff?" Penny had parked at the curb outside Beauty World and Spa, Allen's girlfriend's shop.

"Everything about me is made up," Penny said. "I'm self-made. You got a problem with that?"

Swindell, who sat in back beside Jenkins, said, "You look like Pauley Perrette, the Goth girl on NCIS. You ever get that from people?"

"You think so?" Penny said into the mirror. Her fingers rotated the small silver ball below her pierced lip. "I never would have made that connection. She's so fake. They dress her up like a Goth baby doll, miniskirt and space-age platform boots. That ain't me."

"He's complimenting your cleavage," Jenkins said, "trying to get in good. I told him Roderick would kill him if he stepped out of line. But a penis has no ears."

"You're right," Swindell said to Penny. "She's way too goodie-goodie."

"You're such a suck-up," Jenkins said.

"The NCIS writers stole her from Sean Young, Rachel in *Blade Runner*. That's Ridley Scott, 1982."

"Roderick's gonna cut you into little bitty pieces, Swindell."

"Those women can't wear the metal like me," Penny said. "They lack commitment."

Allen, the guy inside his girlfriend's beauty shop, had brought Penny on board because the plan was to fake a car theft, which required a second driver. Plus, they'd need a ride at the end of the job after Allen torched the car they weren't really stealing. Plus-plus, having a woman along, one who looked like Penny, would solve the problem that a police lineup might present. All eyes turned when Penny entered the picture. She would not be present for the job itself.

"I like 'em," Swindell said. "They're like signatures of your individuality. You should have lived in England in the '80s."

"Dead man walking," Jenkins said, slouching lower in the back seat, allowing the derby to rest on the bridge of his nose.

"I'm taking back that hat if you keep dissin' me," Swindell said to Jenkins. He spoke to Penny in the mirror. "He can't appreciate a gift. I bought it for the job cause I thought it'd make him look like Malcolm McDowell in *A Clockwork Orange*. That's Stanley Kubrick, 1971."

"Hat's mine now," Jenkins said. "Finders keepers, losers weepers."

"How many piercings you got?" Swindell said to Penny.

"Twenty-one," Penny said. "Got number twenty-one on my twenty-first birthday."

Jenkins thumped up the derby and leaned way forward so that he could see over the seat. "I don't see near that many," Jenkins said.

"Most ain't for public viewing," Penny said.

"Roderick like 'em?" Swindell said.

"You're *such* a suckdog, Swindell."

Allen had brought on thin-faced Jenkins only because Allen had thrown out his back. Swindell was Allen's regular side.

"We're done, the two of us, him and me," Penny said. "Roderick said my labia looked like a pin cushion."

"What did *you* say?" Swindell said.

"I said to him, 'Call me Pin then. Pin is mightier than the sword,' I said."

Jenkins said, "I'll show you something mightier than the sword."

"Be like trying to put a marshmallow in a parking meter," Penny said.

"So is Penny your real name?" Swindell said.

"Nothing about me is real," Penny said.

Jenkins rolled a joint from a small bag of stems and seeds. "Does Allen even know we're out here waiting?" he said.

"Allen's the one said this was time sensitive," Swindell said. "Maybe we should knock on the door." The three exchanged looks. "Maybe not," Swindell said.

***

Allen was lying naked on the masseuse's table with his fingertips soaking in a saucer of Trish's special nail-softening solution. Trish was working on Allen's lower back. "I could take out most of your grey, maybe just leave the hi-lights," Trish said. Trish was a professional cosmetologist. But she'd begun classes at Florence-Darlington Technical College to certify in massage therapy.

"Look outside and see if there's a black four-door Maxima with a Dough-Dough's Pizza sign on top," Allen said.

Trish lifted her oily hands from Allen's back. "I'm naked," she said. "Somebody might see me."

"Take a look," Allen said.

Trish cradled her breasts in her forearms as she tiptoed to the front door of the shop and peeked over the sign that said closed. A young woman with coal black hair sat at the wheel and two men, one wearing a funny hat, in the back.

"What's the deal with the pizza sign on top of the car?" Trish said. She and Allen were getting dressed.

"It's like a master key," Allen said. "You can go anywhere with a pizza sign. Nobody asks questions."

"How's the back?" she said. She handed him a slip of paper with Rupert's number on it. "Any better?"

"Better after this job's done," Allen said. He pressed a folded fifty into her palm and kissed her.

Outside, Allen waddled toward the car then leaned gingerly into the passenger seat. "What's up with the derby," he said.

"Malcolm McDowell, *A Clockwork Orange*, 1971," thin-faced Jenkins said. He gave Swindell a big wink, smiled broadly and patted the top of the hat.

"Stan Laurel, *Dirty Work*, 1933," Allen said. "Let's get this show on the road. Stop at Walgreens."

"We're already running behind," Penny said. She looked over at Allen, who looked down at his perfect fingernails.

***

On the drive to Walgreens, Swindell asked if a frozen body would float like an ice cube does. He reckoned that it would if the body was frozen soon after death.

"Frozen hard?" Jenkins said.

"Hard as a brick," Swindell said.

"If you put a brick in the freezer, will it float, Swindell?" Jenkins said.

"What's your opinion?" Penny said to Allen.

"If we don't get to where we're going soon, we'll never know," Allen said.

She parked out front. "Walgreens?" Penny said.

"They got TracFones for $14.99," Allen said. "Plus, I got a super-saver's coupon." Allen held up the evidence of his savings.

"This where Rupert buys his disposables?"

"If he's thrifty, he does." Allen said.

Jenkins, Swindell and Penny sat up tall as Allen stepped out from the electronic door and into the July afternoon light. He lifted a slip of paper from his shirt pocket, looked down at his new phone and dialed a number, then turned his back to them.

"You're late," Rupert barked on the other end.

"We're leaving Walgreens now," Allen said. "They've got a hell of a deal on these phones."

Inside the car, Jenkins said to Penny, "Are your nipples pierced?" Penny paid him no mind. "They are, aren't they? Both of them."

"I left the headlights on," Rupert said to Allen. "But I've been waiting for thirty minutes. My shopping cart's half full already."

"Didn't you pack the fish on dry ice?"

"Yes."

"Then we'll be all right."

"It's hot out there, Allen. Get a move on."

Allen said, "Don't forget to keep your receipt, Rupert."

"What?"

"When you reenter the store to report the car stolen, you'll need a receipt to get a refund."

"How's the back?" Rupert said.

"Hurts like a muther," Allen said.

"That's too bad," Rupert said.

***

Ordinarily, the drive from Darlington to the Super Walmart in Florence is twenty minutes. Twenty-five tops. But not today.

"What's with the traffic?" Allen said.

"Beach traffic," Penny said.

"Today's July fourth," Swindell said, staring down into his cell. Jenkins lit a joint. Allen waved it off.

"Did you smoke pot back in the day?" Swindell said, taking the joint from Jenkins. "*Reefer?*"

"In the late sixties and through the seventies," Allen said. "I quit when the music started to suck."

Swindell said, "Damn, Allen." He nodded thanks to the joint then passed it up to Penny. "You were there for all the great movies. *Five Easy Pieces, The Last Picture Show. Straw Dogs?* That's my favorite. How 'bout you? What's your favorite?"

"*Bonnie and Clyde*, 1967," Allen said.

"Never cared for that one so much," Swindell said. "I mean you know how it's gonna end."

"That's why I like it," Allen said.

They crossed Palmetto Street. Up ahead, traffic had come to a stop. "What the hell?" Jenkins said. Soon they realized they were trapped at the tail end of a bicycle race. The side streets were blocked off.

Penny looked down into her phone. "Text from Roderick," she said. "Now he wants to make up."

"What does it say?" Swindell asked.

"'Why don't you hurry and get off the rack, I can't wait to get you back in the sack. Signed, The Poet, Romeo Rod.' He just wants sex," she said.

Jenkins said, "The dentist never warned him to keep sharp metal objects out of his mouth?"

Allen looked at his TracFone. Rupert had called. He didn't need to hear the message to know what it was.

They were creeping along now. Jenkins spoke to Penny. "Who do you think enjoys sex more, men or women?"

"Women."

"I don't think so," he said.

Penny sighed and struck a theatrical pose for the rearview. "Put your finger in your ear, Jenkins," she said. "Now, which feels better, your finger or your ear?"

"You really should have been an actress," Swindell said. "You'd be rich."

"Never wanted to be an actress. I wanted to be a singer. In a punk band. Not that phony stuff, though. A real '80s punk-punk band."

"What would you name your group?" Swindell said.

"The Pussy Farts," she said.

"*Killer*," Swindell said.

Jenkins studied the cluster of cyclists up ahead. "You'd think they'd get the hell out of the way. Look at those outfits. Those helmets. They look like a swarm of locusts. They're all so skinny and gay. I wouldn't be caught dead dressed like that. Look at that guy. He's wearing padded stretch pants."

Soon the bicyclists began dispersing. The side streets opened and the riders began peeling off. "Make a detour," Allen said. "Step on it." Penny turned onto National Cemetery Road. She slowed for a stop sign beside a rider who sat waiting to cross. Jenkins looked over at Swindell and slowly wagged his head from side to side in contempt. He rolled down his window.

"Nice butt, sweetheart," he crooned.

The skinny man on the bicycle, who was only a couple a feet away, slowly, mechanically, turned and looked at Jenkins. "Takes a real faggot to spot a nice looking guy," he said.

Jenkins opened his door. The instant his foot touched the pavement, the rider jerked up his knee and kung fu kicked the car door into Jenkin's shin. "Ahhhhh!" he shouted, reflexively falling forward to grab the leg. Jenkins' derby toppled onto the street, leaving his high-piled brown curls looking like a chocolate cupcake. In the next second, the rider jerked a fistful of hair and slammed his hip against the car door, bam-bam-bam, hammering Jenkins' head against the door jam. Then the rider flipped his bicycle in the opposite direction and was gone. It all happened—wham! Just like that. Swindell heaved Jenkins back into the car. "Drive," Allen said.

Jenkins was moaning and babbling incoherently, his swollen bleeding head rolling about his shoulders like a marble in a shot glass. "Damn," Swindell said to Allen. "He looks like Gene Hackman in that scene from *Bonnie and Clyde*, when half Buck Barrow's head's been blown off, don't he?"

Allen's phone rang again. "I got a bad, bad feeling," Rupert said.

"We're pulling in the Walmart lot now," Allen said.

"I got two carts of merchandise," Rupert said. "That's one too many. Every worker here has seen my face three times. Quintin called."

"I'm looking for the car right now," Allen said.

"One with the headlights on, I told you."

"I don't see it."

"Ancient Gold Mercedes, size of an aircraft carrier."

Penny circled the outer perimeter of the lot.

"There," Allen said.

"I don't see any headlights," Penny said.

"That's got to be it."

Two rows over, Penny parked as Swindell tucked the tools he'd need into his back pocket then pulled his shirttail down to cover them. She watched as he and Allen climbed into the front seat of the gold car. In the seat behind her, Not-thin-faced Jenkins laid writhing and moaning, speaking in tongues.

Within a minute, Allen was crossing the lot back toward her, huffing with every painful step. He opened his wallet as he neared her window. Penny said, "Problem with the ignition?"

"No," Allen said. "Battery's dead. Here." He handed her three fifties. "Go inside to automotive. Buy an adjustable wrench. Tell the guy you need a battery for a Mercedes." He handed her a piece of paper. "Car's model number," he said.

"We got a problem," Penny said.

"That's what I'm telling you," Allen said.

"Look," she said. Allen turned. Water was dripping from the trunk of the battered gold car.

"Hurry," he said.

Penny stood in Auto beside an obese woman on a motorized scooter. Twice Penny had pressed the button for customer assistance, and her patience was a little thin. She was eyeballing the rack of batteries and fingering the ball of the piercing below her lip when the very large woman, whose mass flowed like lava from the scooter, spoke to her.

"Are those real?" she said.

Penny opened her mouth and pulled on the beaded silver

head.

"No, I meant your tits," the woman said.

Penny bowed breast-to-eye-level and pulled her top down a couple of inches, enough to show a pierced nipple.

"Oh, Jesus, child!" the woman said. The electric scooter lurched forward, the weight of its cargo creating a rippling tsunami effect upon the woman's abundant flesh. The scooter and its driver vanished like camouflage into the other shoppers.

Penny looked up and down the aisle. She flagged a young, tall black man. "That one she said. The biggest one." The man lifted the heavy battery and set it in her cart.

"You Roderick's girl, ain't you?"

"How do you know that?" Penny said.

"Ain't a lot of girls look like you," he said.

Rupert spotted her as she made for the checkouts. He was half a foot shorter than Penny, his nicotine-ravaged face knotted sinew, his depleted body wiry and furtive. When he spoke, he weaved and darted like a featherweight boxer. "You tell Allen that if this goes bad, he goes down. Can you remember that?"

"I think so," Penny said.

"Get the hell out of here."

She looked at his two overflowing carts. "Don't forget to keep your receipt," she said.

Swindell was under the hood of the Mercedes when Penny wheeled the battery outside. She didn't see Allen. "Where is he?" she said to Swindell.

"Lying in the backseat. This the right battery?"

"Biggest one they got," Penny said. She stopped at the window of the Mercedes and spoke to Allen. "How is it?" she said.

"Like somebody's holding a blowtorch to the nerve," Allen said, gently pulling himself up. "We'll switch out the battery. You head on to the Cashua Ferry landing. Call if there's a problem on that end."

"I'll take Pocket Road," she said.

"Don't let Jenkins fall asleep," Allen said. "If somebody other than us happens to show up at the landing, crawl in the back and pretend you're screwing."

"He's got the moaning part down," she said.

"Did Rupert see you?" Allen asked. Penny didn't have to

answer. "Time," Allen said. "When you get old, like me, you'll know time is the real enemy."

"Rupert's learning that now," Penny said. "He picked up a bunch of frozen foods. I saw it dripping from the bottom of his cart. I told him to keep his receipt, but they might not refund thawed beef ribs."

"Right. They might exercise a little prerogative, a little free will," Allen said.

"I don't believe in free will," Penny said. "I'm Pentecostal."

"Hear that ticking," Allen said. He meant the rapid dripping from the trunk.

"Like a clock," Penny said.

"Or a time bomb," Allen said, reaching for the headrest and slowly, painfully heaving himself up. He watched Penny's skinny-girl-with-big-tits walk.

Allen called to her. "Lose the pizza sign."

"I don't think this is the right battery," Swindell said from under the hood.

"Got to make it work," Allen said, trudging slowly.

"What's that smell?" Swindell said.

"Don't ask," Allen said.

"I want to try something before I change out batteries just to make sure the problem ain't in the switch. Wrong battery could blow the whole electrical system. We'd be stuck."

"Okay," Allen said.

Under the hood, Swindell located the car's "convenience center" and inside it the fuse box. His plan was to ground the starter relay and hopefully start the car. But he was working from the terminal side of the box and inadvertently hit the accessory maxi fuse. He and Allen heard the sizzle and saw the thin coil of black smoke rise. "Oops," Swindell said.

"Try the battery," Allen said.

***

Allen lifted his foot from the accelerator and the heavy car slowed to a creep.

"What are you doing?" Swindell said. The gold Mercedes glided past the main entrance of the Super Walmart, where they saw Rupert inside, tugging the two carts toward the checkout.

"Just like I thought," Allen said. "The son of a bitch is gonna report the car stolen before we get to the Darlington County line."

"How much time does that give us?" Swindell said.

"Depends on how long it takes the cops to respond, do the paperwork, radio a description of the car."

"It'll take the checkout person forever to issue his refund. He'll give us time," Swindell said. "He has to."

"Yeah," Allen said. "That's what we'll get all right. Thirty years, I'd guess."

"Rupert, he's just scared, that's all," Swindell said.

"Ain't that a plenty?" Allen said. He stopped for the light then looked down at the dash. "Problem," he said. "The turn signals are blown."

They took National Cemetery Road behind the airport and out to Highway 327. From there it was a straight shot to Seven Bridges Road and the old Cashua Ferry Landing, where Penny and Jenkins were waiting. If Jenkins was conscious, he and Swindell would quickly toss the body into the Great Pee Dee River. Allen, followed by Penny, would drive the Mercedes to Mullins thirty miles away and torch it in a field of abandoned cars. Penny would deliver the team like pizzas to their safe homes. It was already a little past seven, but there was more than an hour of sunlight left, time to finish the job.

The throb in Allen's lower back forced him into constant motion, and he rocked like a lunatic. "I got to look for some other line of work," he said to Swindell, who was mesmerized by the phone he stared into. "My back is killing me. You, you'll go blind before your back goes out." He motioned toward Swindell's phone. "Your kids will look like Martians, scrawny little fingers for texting, extra-large eyes for seeing the miniature screen."

Swindell didn't look up. "And big ole bubble heads," he said. "E.T., 1982."

"Yeah," Allen said. "Like Jenkins' head is looking about now."

"That's the future," Swindell said.

"The future," Allen said. "It never lasts."

"I got me a million dollar idea for the future," Swindell said. "Couple of years, I'll retire." He affected even more of a Southern accent: "Two ways to get rich Rhett But-la says in *Gone With The Wind*, that would be 1939. When a civilization is bein' built and when it's bein' destroyed. Ain't much doubt about which track we're on." His thumbs moved at lightning speed.

"What's your idea?" Allen said. They were approaching the intersection of I-95, and beyond that smooth sailing.

"To apply old technology to future needs. Steve Jobs," Swindell said. "Here's the old technology: water mill. Water turns the wheel. Wheel generates energy. New technology?" He held up his phone. "This device requires electricity. Electricity requires fossil fuels, which are running out."

"What will you do without your little computer?" Allen said.

"Without it? I will die. And not just me. This here is *life*, man."

"Some life," Allen said. His back was killing him. Just ahead at the intersection, the light turned. He heard the shift of the body in the trunk as he came to a stop. A state trooper's car faced them in the westbound lane. Allen checked his watch. Shift change, he thought. "Sounds like a done deal. So how do you propose to go on living after your machines die?"

"Simple," Swindell said. "Inside the human body, you implant an artificial vein and artery to the chambers of the heart, simple plumbing job, and run the lines so that they come out about here." He pointed to the underside of his left wrist. "You have an import jack that fits into one side of the phone, where the blood enters, and an export jack on the other side, sending blood back to the heart."

"Your phone is connected to your heart?"

"More of an extension of your heart, I'd say. And so you have this little wheel, like a water mill, inside the phone, see, and with every heartbeat, that wheel turns, which generates a low electrical signal, enough to power the phone. And there you have it. Eternal life for as long as you live."

"Heaven, huh?" Allen said.

"As close to it as you and I are likely to get," Swindell said.

Passing the intersection of Highway 327 and Pocket Road, a late model pickup pulled out behind the Mercedes, its driver a young, chiseled-faced man with a buzz cut. The truck followed at the legal distance for three miles, to a stop sign at Seven Bridges

Road. The driver noticed that the Mercedes had no brake lights, and as the big golden car came to a stop, the conscientious driver lightly tapped his horn. Swindell glanced over at Allen, who was looking into his side mirror. The driver opened his door and started toward the Mercedes. Allen saw the reflected red flicker of sunset in the man's badge.

"That ain't a trooper's car," Swindell announced in genuine surprise.

"Don't mean he ain't got a scanner," Allen said. When Allen bent forward, a current of pain shot up his spine, one so sharp and intense that he winced. His eyes watered. When his vision cleared, he shot the man in the face.

They were less than two miles from the old ferry landing.

***

The Mercedes' brakes shrieked bare metal down the steep, narrow path to the river. Penny's black Maxima sat parked off to the side. Allen eked his way out of the driver's side, very slowly straightened up and pressed his back against the car. His face was covered in sweat.

"Whose brains you wearing?" Penny said. Allen didn't answer. He dug into his pocket for folding money. Allen handed the money to Swindell, who had stepped around to inspect the stained driver's side of the car, but he spoke to Penny. "Y'all go back to Walmart. Buy a flashlight, a pack of bath towels and some rubber gloves like you use to clean the oven, a gallon of bleach, a spinning rod and everything I'll need for catching catfish. And a bottle of Motrin I B."

"Twenty pound test line?" Swindell asked.

"Twenty pound ought to do it," Allen said. "And beer. A six-pack for me and whatever y'all want."

"What about him?" Swindell said. Jenkins was asleep in the backseat of the Maxima, his head looking a little like the cork of a champagne bottle.

"He won't be waking up any time soon, if at all," Allen said.

He fanned a swarming cloud of mosquitoes from around his face as he watched the red taillights of the Maxima climb the rutted drive and vanish under the canopy of water oaks and pines. Allen knew that he'd have to stay put until first light. The plan had been to erase any connection between the car and the body. The Mercedes had no headlights. Torching the car at the landing was too risky, as was tossing the body into the dark river. "July fourth," he said aloud, thinking that maybe the holiday would work in his favor. Nobody in his right mind would spend the night of the fourth in a place like this, he thought.

He tried lying flat on his back, which was a mistake. Getting down and up again was torture. The searing pain tore through him like a hot wire, one terminal just below the shoulder blade, its charged voltage firing down his back and through his buttocks to the opposite terminal in his scrotum. Heaving deep breaths, Allen shuffled to the rear of the Mercedes, then, transferring as much weight as he could, pressed his palms on the hot trunk lid, beneath which laid a soft heap of gooey, grey mush. His phone rang. He fanned away the flies and looked down at the lighted number. But he didn't answer.

***

"I'll hold the flashlight. You tie on that swivel for me," Allen said to Swindell. "I can't see for shit." Swindell was assembling the fishing rod while Penny set the other supplies in the backseat of the Mercedes. Allen opened a beer and shook four Motrin into his palm.

Swindell said, "Me and Penny have been talking, Allen. One of us has to have a meeting with Rupert. Phone's been ringing off the hook."

"Ain't no hook no more," Allen said.

"You know what we're talking about," Penny said. "Rupert's got to know, on account of Quentin. And we got bills to pay."

"You can forget about anybody getting paid," Allen said. "What's your plan?"

"Rupert's scared," Swindell said. "Somebody's got to calm him down."

"How calm do you suppose he's got to be to keep his mouth shut?" A sudden raging chorus of tree frogs devoured Allen's words. The three exchanged glancing looks. Then all was quiet except for the constant hum of mosquitos and the soft lapping of the river's tide.

"As calm as a man can be," Penny said.

"Somebody's got to insure Rupert's eternal tranquility," Swindell said.

"'Eternal tranquility.' That would be Swindell, 2012," Allen said.

Swindell passed the fishing rod he had readied over to Allen. "Thanks a lot," Allen said.

***

For him, there was no standing and there was no sitting, no lying down. Instead, he discovered that leaning against a cyprus at the water's edge was the most comfort he could find. After a second round of extra strength pain relievers, he bleached the inside of the Mercedes, the outside of the doors, its hood and trunk. When the pain became unbearable, he tossed his rags into the river and picked up his spinning rod. As the night bled out, he watched the darkness slowly descend into the river. He didn't get a bite all night.

***

Surgeon-like, Allen pulled on the yellow oven-cleaning gloves and took his agony by the inch as he slowly slid behind the wheel. He drove the Seven Bridges Road north to I-95 then double backed south to I-20 and west to Camden. From the main drag off the interstate, he turned onto De Kalb and followed it to Heratio Gates Estates and to Freedom Drive, the quiet winding street to Rupert's condo. On his approach, Allen noted that Rupert's balcony overlooked the water hazard of a par three.

He parked the Mercedes beside the only SUV in the lot and tucked the gloves into his back pocket. He left the engine idling.

Allen knocked, then pressed his palm over the peep hole, hoping Rupert would piss his pants. "Who is it?" Rupert said in a trembling sing-song voice.

"Pizza delivery," Allen said.

Rupert fell away from the open door, laid back his head against the wall and shut his eyes. "Jesus," he jeered, his breath reeking of whiskey.

"If you smell something that stinks," Allen said, "it's just the cheese in the trunk." He gave Rupert the "come hither" finger motion.

Rupert's eyes went cat-in-a-toilet. He staggered back then lunged for the door. Too late. Allen was there. "Mother of god," Rupert moaned. "Oh, Jesus, Allen." Allen stepped into the condo.

"I'll leave my shoes here, on the mat," he said. "I'd hate to soil the carpet."

Rupert retreated a step, then held his ground. "What's happening here?" he said with a lift of the chin. He inflated his thin chest. "What the fuck's that car doing in my lot? This is your problem. Now it's between you and Quentin. Nothing I can do for you, Allen."

"What you can do for me—for really both of us, Rupert—is pour us a glass of whiskey. I'm thirsty and my back really hurts. That is if you don't mind. What's happening is what I'm here to talk to you about. But first, let's you and me take a little spin around the block."

"I ain't going nowhere with you," Rupert said.

Allen looked down into the plush carpet, took a slow, deep, tortured breath. He griped the pistol in his back pocket. His red eyes inched up to meet Rupert's. Every step up to the condo had felt like having a nail driven into his back. "Yes, Rupert." Allen nodded. "I think you are."

Going down the stairs was easier, but not by much. "Open my door for me," Allen said.

"I ain't your chauffeur," Rupert said.

"Come on," Allen said. "My back is killing me."

To straighten his legs, Allen had set the driver's seat all the way back, and now Rupert looked like a dwarf as he stretched for the pedals.

"Where you headed?" Allen said.

"The interstate," Rupert said. "I know where this ends. Don't insult me, Allen."

"No way," Allen said. "You're drunk. You'll get us both arrested. We'll just do the residential tour, have a quiet little chat."

Rupert drove slowly. Allen sat with his hands in his lap. "What went wrong?" Rupert said.

"You got scared," Allen said.

"Well, I ain't scared now," Rupert said.

"Explain that puddle of piss you're sitting in."

"Ha. Ha," Rupert said. "I ain't scared 'cause I know how this ends."

"No, you don't. Turn around."

"What's going on here?"

Back at Rupert's condo, Allen stopped just inside the door. "Do me a favor," he said to Rupert. "Take off my shoes."

"Fuck you," Rupert said.

Allen lifted his shirt and pulled the thick yellow rubber gloves from one pocket and the .22 Ruger from the other. "Pretty please," he said.

***

Rupert brought whiskey and two glasses from the kitchen. Allen stood barefoot beside the dining room table where he could watch him.

"Sit," Allen said. "Me, I've got to stand." Allen poured tall glasses of bourbon. They both drank. Then Allen poured another glass for Rupert. "Drink," Allen said.

"I'm already drunk," Rupert slurred. Allen pointed the pistol at the glass and Rupert lifted it to his lips. Allen shook out four Motrin tablets, downed the pills with the last of his drink.

"You ever had back trouble?" Allen said.

"Yeah," Rupert said. "In the navy."

"How bad?" Allen said. "You never had it like this."

"Bad," Rupert said. "Flat on my back. No sex for six weeks."

"That's cause you didn't have a girlfriend."

"I had plenty."

"What'd you do, pick all the ones without hands?"

"What do you know about girlfriends, old fuck like you?"

"Drink," Allen said.

"I don't want no more. I'm blind now."

"Yes, you do want some more," Allen said.

Rupert nodded at the pistol in Allen's hand. "I know how this ends," he said. "I don't want no more."

"You don't know how this ends, and you do want some more." Allen slid the glass a little closer to Rupert. "Long as you're drinking, you're breathing." Allen held the glass up to Rupert's lips. "Here's to your health," he said. Rupert drank. Allen poured again.

"You ain't never had a girlfriend." Rupert's words came out in little stuttered syllables.

"Got one now," Allen said. "Cosmetologist who's studying to do massage. I got the whole package. Hair, nails and a back rub."

Rupert's chin kept colliding with is chest. "You got a fuckin' woman who studies the universe?"

"No," Allen said. "Cosmetologist. Drink up."

"And gives you a fuckin' back rub?" Rupert began that gyroscope action where his upper body moved in wider and wider circles while his butt somehow remained attached to the seat of his chair. "And you've fucked her?"

"Many times," Allen said. "Drink up, Rupert."

"You time fucker, you," Rupert said lifting his glass. "But you got to pay her for the back rubs, don't you?" Allen didn't answer. "You don't have a girlfriend, Allen. You never had a girlfriend. What you got's a whore. A whore's all you've ever had. I think I'm gonna vomit."

"I think so, too," Allen said.

Rupert slowly stood, holding his arms outstretched for balance like a tightrope artist. He stumbled toward the bathroom. "I'd hate to throw up on the carpet," he mumbled.

"I'd hate it, too," Allen said.

Rupert dropped to his knees then with mighty heaves gushed into the toilet. Allen slowly tick-tocked in behind him, pulling on the heavy yellow gloves. He knotted Rupert's hair into his fist, lifting his head. "Go," Allen instructed. Rupert tossed down the front of his shirt and pants. "Oops," Allen said. "Now we got to get you out of these clothes." Rupert lay motionless on the floor while Allen ran him a good hot bath.

The effort required to lift Rupert into the tub brought tears to Allen's eyes and took his breath. Panting and sweating, he sat now on the cool tile floor resting against the tub while fiery spasms of electric pain crawled over his back like giant venomous spiders. He lifted an exhausted arm and felt inside the tub for Rupert's face. He pressed down until the bubbles stopped. Allen glanced back when Rupert's hand touched his arm. But there was no resistance there, just a slow wave, a bye-bye.

He poured himself a drink and hobbled out to Rupert's balcony. Below, the surface of the par three's water hazard was calm. He drank and then lobbed the glass into the pond. Across the way he heard the light tap of a car horn. The Dough-Dough's Pizza sign made the car easy to spot.

***

Allen braced himself, arms spread, hands against the wall, legs spread, eyes closed. Trish tenderly undressed him. She guided him onto the masseuse's table and then brought steaming towels. She lit a candle. The room smelled of cucumber. In silence, she slowly orbited him, her strong knowing hands exorcising the poison from body and spirit. When she massaged his neck, her soft, naked breasts brushed his aching back. "You're gonna have to give this time," Trish said.

Allen closed his eyes. He had bought some time for him and Penny and Swindell. Then he considered the absurd notion of "buying time." The only thing certain about time was that it ran out. There was a chance that without a motive the cops might never make the connection between events in Camden and Florence. Most certainly Camden cops would be scratching their heads to figure the connection between the drunk who drowned in his tub and whose prints were found in a stolen Mercedes with a dead man in its trunk. Maybe Penny would marry Roderick and live a happy life and Swindell would patent his revolutionary blood phone and become rich. Maybe Jenkins would discover a kind word. But these were not endings. These were the in-betweens. Those clumsy gestures between the tenuous now and the certain then.

"I can't tell you what this means to me," Allen whispered. Trish's hands were slowly wringing the poison from his muscles.

"Sure you can," Trish said. Allen smiled. "Go ahead, sweet-talk me," she said.

"I don't have the words," he said, again closing his eyes, again feeling the pain seep from him.

"It's cause I'm naked, ain't it, Allen? My stunning middle-aged beauty leaves you mute, don't it?"

"Yes, it does."

"Liar," she said.

Allen watched the flicker of the flame, the slow demise of the candle.

Trish drizzled more warm oil and gently worked it in.

"How's that?" she said.
"Heaven," Allen said. "Heaven."

From the UV Files

File #77
GARY CLIFTON

Cruel and Unusual

Hunters found the first victim in a fence row, Janice Bradford, 10, missing three days, nude, beaten, raped, mutilated. She'd last been seen being dropped off at a school bus in front of her rural home. Benton County Sheriff Glen Shepherd, a retired 20 year Marine Gunnery Sergeant, with more lines in his face than a map of Arkansas, examined the scene. He ordered the body transported to the DPS lab, Austin for forensic examination.

Shepherd, a robust fifty-five, was well known among west Central Texas criminals as a tough customer, but a fair man. Shepherd instinctively saw that the brutality of the crime, the remoteness of Benton County and lack of manpower would make investigation urgent and difficult.

The lab confirmed the rape, identified teeth marks on the mangled body and added a kicker: Janice had been run over by a car, had paint specks on her forehead and had been shot behind the ear with a .22.

A week later, a farmer stumbled across little Rose Minelli, 9, missing a week, nude and battered, in his hay barn, two miles from the first crime scene. She also had last been seen getting off a rural school bus.

The lab examined the second body. The connection was obvious. Rose had also been hit by a car, possibly while trying to run and shot in the back of her head with a .22. Spectrographic analysis indicated the paint flecks were from the same model car: an older Dodge Dart. Both girls were shot with the same firearm.

Shepherd, grasping at air, examined the records of every merchant who sold .22 ammunition within fifty miles. Federal law at the time required purchasers of .22 ammunition to produce a valid ID and sign for the cartridges.

In a week, he'd accumulated enough names to fill a pickup truck bed. Well aware chances of success were less than thin, Shepherd sent two female secretaries to Austin to cross-check the names/licenses with persons owning an older Dodge Dart who had any history of sex or child molestation crimes.

Then, by the luck of non-believers, Charlie Beasley, 20, who'd bought a box of .22 ammo at a rural gas station and who owned a Dodge Dart, had been arrested for indecent exposure three months earlier. The case had been dropped. Charlie lived with his mother less than five miles from both crime scenes.

Shepherd rounded Beasley up. A scrawny, snotty, little weasel with a wisp of hair showing an unsuccessful attempt at raising a mustache; his greasy hair hung in clumps. In five minutes, Shepherd saw Beasley was guilty and needed killing, but the law, even in rural Texas, no longer allowed that.

"Mama allays said them little girls was dirty," he sneered. "I never touched them little bitches. Gimme a cigarette, hick cop."

"Charlie, I know you cruise them roads in that old Dart ever' day," Shepherd drawled. "Got witnesses saw you near both girl's houses. We got deputies out at your mama's right now with a search warrant. We find that .22, it goes up your ass."

Confronted with the paint samples and the .22 ammo purchase, Charlie smirked.

Texas law at the time, required that any confession to Texas officers to be admitted in a Texas court proceeding, had to be in writing and sworn before a judge. Charlie wasn't about to sign anything. When the search warrant team returned without a gun, Shepherd knew the case was temporarily in the toilet. Charlie had stashed the gun. He released Charlie and immediately formed Plan B.

Shepherd located the complainant in the earlier indecent exposure incident, Ella Fletcher, 61, a farm homemaker. "Walked past that old Dodge on the Safeway parking lot. Little animal settin' in there...unzipped his pants and showed me his...thing. The husband said not to file no charges."

Shepherd had a come-to-Jesus talk with Ella Fletcher's husband the same morning. Shepherd had an arrest warrant for Charlie Beasley in an hour and had Charlie in jail in two.

Shepherd strolled through the cellblock which housed around twenty inmates. Two or three catcalls rang out, but several other prisoners, familiar with Shepherd's no bullshit, but fair treatment, greeted him through the bars. He walked back through the turn-key and asked the jailer to bring him two prisoners by name. Then he made a deal with two inmates awaiting trial for rape and with the Devil.

Around midnight, the night jailer called Shepherd out of bed. "Charlie Beasley says he's ready to confess."

When Shepherd parked his pickup in front of the old house, he could hear a shrieking voice from outside the building. By the time he entered the upstairs jail, he recognized Charlie's wailing screams: "Too deep! For Christ's sake, no more...too deep."

"I'm alone here," the jailer said. "Sheriff, you better handle this."

Shepherd dragged Charlie into an interview room, his trousers torn and bloody, the stench of feces overpowering. Shepherd pushed a yellow pad and pencil across the table.

"How long you think your asshole is gonna hold out, tough guy." Shepherd turned to walk out.

"Wait, wait," Charlie squealed, probably Shepherd thought, much like his two little victims.

"Start writin', Charlie."

On Charlie's confession, they dragged the .22 pistol from the Brazos River. Ballistics were a match to both girls' wounds. The DPS lab matched the paint flecks from the victims' heads to Charlie's Dodge. Charlie Beasley was executed at Huntsville three years later. The courts and newspapers danced on and around the issue of cruel and unusual punishment for months, but Charlie's complaints never grew legs. Who'd believe an animal like Charlie Beasley?

"Cruel and Unusual treatment, you think?" Shepherd always responded. "Seen the crime photos? When we go to hell, I'll explain the whole deal there."

File #80
NICK MEDINA

Caged

Each scratch on the wall equaled one day spent in the cell. There were thousands there; some so old that they were barely distinguishable in the concrete.

Jack Nestler had been sentenced in the seventies. He knew that for sure, but he couldn't remember the year, and certainly not the day. Everything seemed to blur as soon as the judge dropped the gavel. And letting life blur became Nestler's way of surviving. Call it bad luck, being in the wrong place at the wrong time, or fate, but Jack called his turn in life, false imprisonment.

"Nestler!" Officer Anderson barked from outside Jack's bars. "What are you doing under there?"

Jack popped his head out from beneath his bunk. "Counting," he said.

Anderson sneered at him. Jack had been a model prisoner. He'd never caused trouble and he never took part in it either. Put together, those two things were precisely why Officer Anderson didn't trust the man; that and the fact that Nestler was two days from freedom and he still hadn't owned up to what he'd done.

Jack didn't sleep that night. He'd counted over eight-thousand marks on the wall before lights out, and as he lay there on the mattress that'd gone flat years ago, he realized he wouldn't get through all the marks before being set free. There were just too many; each one representing wasted time, dreadful repetition and humiliating persistence. If anything, Jack was persistent.

It was raining when the sun came up. Jack's first thought was that he only had one night left. For as long as he could remember he had insisted that he didn't belong behind bars, and yet, when it came down to it, he couldn't imagine waking up anywhere else.

"Back against the bars," Officer Anderson, accompanied by two others, grumbled from outside Nestler's cell.

Jack complied, cooperative as ever. The men led him away, and before he knew it he was in a great, ugly room with the warden himself.

"You'll be going tomorrow," the warden told him.

"Yes, sir," Jack agreed.

"How do you feel?"

Jack's lower lip trembled. "Excited, I guess," he said.

"I want you to know that I'm proud of you."

"Thank you, sir."

"You've been an exemplary prisoner, a real role model for the others."

Jack thanked him again.

"You've paid your debt to society," the warden went on. "As far as I'm concerned what you did—"

"I didn't do it," Jack interjected.

The warden's face frazzled and then turned stern. "You can't keep saying that," he explained. "Not after how you hurt her."

***

Jack sat juddering, trembling like a child in the snow, while his final hour as a property of the state ticked away.

"What are ya shakin' for?" one of the guards asked. "You ain't goin' to the chair. You're goin' back to the real world."

The real world, Jack thought. As firmly as he believed that he didn't deserve to be surrounded by the impenetrable concrete and steel, the prison was the only world he really knew.

"Take me back," he blurted. "I forgot something in my cell."

"Your cell's clean. It'll be someone else's soon enough," the officer said.

Jack got mad at that. It was his cell. He was the one who spent over thirty years wasting away in it. It was where he'd given up hope, where he lost his youth and where he assumed he would die.

"What's the first thing you're gonna do out there?" the guard asked.

Jack shrugged.

"Aww, come on now. Ain't you been plannin' this day for thirty years? There's gotta be somethin' ya wanna do."

"No," Jack muttered.

"Not even with a woman?" the guard prodded.

Jack shook his head. Well into his fifties, he didn't know the ways of a woman. Not really.

"I guess after what ya done you don't wanna—"

"I didn't do it," Jack said once again.

The guard held his hands up in front of him. "Ya don't have to convince me. You're a free man."

The release papers signed and Jack in his civilian clothes, the guards escorted him to a door with a sign over it that he hadn't seen in quite some time.

"Exit," he said, reading.

"Best of luck, Mr. Nestler."

Jack pointed to the door as though he didn't know what it was for.

"Right that way."

Jack let out a heavy breath that sounded like a sob. His stomach churned. He couldn't remember the last time he felt so uncertain. With one last backward glance at the men who once told him what to do and when to do it, he hoisted the box he was taking with him and pushed his way through the door that led to the outside world.

Just like that, he was free. The bars and the barbed wire were behind him. Before him was a crowded parking lot and beyond that a bus stop where he'd been instructed to take the 209 bus to the men's shelter where a room was waiting for him.

"Hello, Jack," a voice said from somewhere to his left.

His head pivoted, bringing him face to face with an old man he somehow recognized. Standing next to the old man was an old woman who looked even more familiar.

"Mom?" he uttered.

She nodded. "Jack, we came for you."

"I didn't want you here."

"We know," his father sighed. "The car's that way." He pointed off in the distance and ambled away.

"It's all right," his mother said. "Everything's going to be okay." She headed for the car herself, peering back just once so that Jack would follow.

Jack had made it crystal clear that he didn't want his parents at the prison. Although they wrote, they hadn't seen one another in over twenty years. Gazing after them now, beholding them as he never had before, a lump formed in his throat. Somehow the picture in his head would have to catch up with the reality before him.

"Come on, Jack," his mother called one last time.

Propelled into motion by woeful wonder more than anything else, Jack stumbled along after the wrinkled bags of bones.

"You can put your things in the trunk," his father said when they reached the car. "And get the door for your mother."

Jack couldn't stop staring. Somewhere beneath the thinning flesh, the age spots and the gray hair were people he once knew. It just took a long time to find them.

"Get in the car, Jack."

"Right," Jack muttered, gently closing the door after his mother got in. It'd been ages since he'd seen a car up close. It'd been even longer since he'd ridden in one without handcuffs around his wrists. He started trembling again.

"The shelter's on Cheltham Street," Jack said as his father pulled away with a box-like device on the dashboard telling him where to turn.

"You're not going to any shelter," his father said.

"We're taking you home," his mother interjected.

Somewhere inside of Jack an argument brewed, but the words never spouted from his lips. Home. His mother said they were taking him home.

***

As with everything else, Jack hadn't seen the red brick bungalow in a very long time. And just like his parents, the house wasn't quite the way he remembered it. The awnings over the windows were faded and worn. The bushes out front were crisp and brown. A crack ran through the concrete stoop. The paint on the garage door had all but chipped away. While everything had deteriorated with age, the mustard yellow curtains hanging in the front window didn't look one bit different. They were as ugly as ever.

"The neighborhood's barely changed," his father remarked. "Mr. and Mrs. Montgomery both passed. Their son Henry lives next door now. You remember Henry, don't you?"

Jack had played with Henry in some other life. "Yeah," he

said.

Mr. and Mrs. Nestler got out of the car before their son. It seemed to Jack that his legs didn't want to move. When he finally got out of the backseat, they felt like warm wax about to give.

"I'll get you a key," Mr. Nestler said upon unlocking the front door.

"You don't have to," Jack said. He'd gotten his box out of the trunk. As light as it was, he didn't think he'd be able to hold it for long.

Mr. Nestler waved a hand through the air. "You'll need a key," he insisted.

The house smelled distinctly of dust, old furniture and decades of home-cooked meals. The place was dim, yet Jack could see the pictures hanging on the walls hadn't changed. The furniture was precisely as it had been the day he left.

"You didn't redecorate?" he wondered.

"Why change?" his father said in reply.

Jack shrugged.

"Your room," Mrs. Nestler cut in, starting down the hall. She tottered along, a slight limp in her step, to the second door on the right.

Jack joined her in the doorway, where he dropped the box from his hands. Suddenly, the sting of tears warmed the corners of his eyes. All his old things were there.

"How old was I when they took me away?"

"Twenty."

"Was I really that young?" he whispered, his eyes falling over the things he once found important: dusty LPs, a baseball trophy, a guitar he never learned to play, stacks of comics. "Why'd you keep everything?"

"Couldn't throw it away, I suppose."

Jack took a seat on the twin bed so that his legs wouldn't give out on him. Surprisingly, the comforter felt familiar even years after he'd forgotten all about it. The feel of it brought a multitude of memories flooding back, some better than others.

"You're probably hungry," Mrs. Nestler said.

Jack started to shake his head, but his mother was on her way to the kitchen long before he could refuse a meal.

So he sat there letting his ghostly memories come back to

life. Everything from the striped wallpaper to the shaggy carpet and the grain of his desk reawakened something in him.

"Your mother's making us something to eat," Mr. Nestler said from the doorway.

"She doesn't have to."

"She wants to."

"I don't have to stay here," he said.

"She wants you to stay."

"I don't understand."

Mr. Nestler gritted his teeth. His eyes fell to the floor. "She believes you," he said. "She doesn't think you did it."

"I didn't do it," Jack insisted.

"I should have baked a cake," Mrs. Nestler said when they were all at the table.

The last thing Jack wanted was a cake. Despite his freedom, the occasion didn't feel like one to be celebrated. He chewed slowly, silently wishing that his mother wouldn't make the moment any more awkward. The uncomfortable silence coming from his father was unbearable enough. Finally he asked, "What is it that you think I'm going to do here?"

After some consideration, Mrs. Nestler carefully dabbed tomato soup away from her lips. "Live," she said.

***

Jack eased into his room after his parents went to bed. The quiet click of the door closing behind him left his ears searching for the cold clang of metal against metal. The room's walls were soft compared to the concrete he'd grown accustomed to.

He flipped the light switch. The lights went out. He flipped it again. The lights came on. He paced. He peered from the window, knowing he could leave if he wanted. He could go anywhere he liked. But then again, he couldn't. Not without being watched, and not without being told to go. Somehow he'd have to figure out how to sleep.

"Rise and shine," Mrs. Nestler said, giving a good rap against Jack's bedroom door the following morning.

Jack lifted his head from the pillow. Rise and shine. It was what his mother said every morning to wake him. For the briefest of instances, he wondered if the past 30 years had all been a dream.

He hopped to the mirror in hopes of seeing his twenty-year-old self. A man steadily slipping down the hill of life, however, looked back at him.

"Jack, aren't you up yet?" Mrs. Nestler called through the door some twenty minutes later.

"Mom..." he said.

She came in. "Breakfast," she said.

"Could you bring it in here?"

"The table's already set."

Jack gulped. "It's just that—" he started.

"Pancakes and eggs," she said, cutting him off. "Your favorite."

Jack's father had the morning paper in front of his face in the kitchen. His mother fixed plates with a smile. It was scary how they were able to pretend that their lives had never been interrupted. They took to breakfast just as they had the day the cops took Jack away. It was as though he'd be leaving for school as soon as he set down his fork. But it wasn't that way at all. When his parents finally saw the truth they'd see that their bodies were failing and that their precious son was a fifty-five-year-old man with an ever-expanding bald spot.

"Let me," Jack said when his mother reached for the dirty dishes.

"Aren't you going out?" Mrs. Nestler asked.

Jack had been given leads to help him secure a job, though the thought of embarking on such a strange and foreign task overwhelmed him. "Not now," he said.

Mr. Nestler lingered at the table with his paper, sipping his coffee every few seconds. Jack had never seen him not head off to work on a weekday before.

"You should let your mother do the dishes," he said. "Makes her feel useful."

"What do you do most days?" Jack asked.

"Whatever I like." He took a loud sip of his coffee.

"What should I do if I don't do the dishes?"

Mr. Nestler shrugged. "You're a free man."

From the UV Files

***

It wasn't until Jack's third day of freedom that he left the house. His mother drove, pointing out the differences in town.

Jack didn't like the store that took the place of the cheery little mart where he bought candy as a kid. It was enormous, and from the second he stepped through its doors it seemed that everyone was looking at him.

"We won't be long," Mrs. Nestler promised. "Do me a favor and find the ground coriander."

Jack hesitated, not knowing where to start. He bypassed an electronics section – bright and beeping with objects he'd only seen in magazines and on television.

"Ground coriander?" he asked a woman in an apron.

She flinched in response. It was a quick and subtle reaction, but Jack was sure he saw it.

"Never mind," he grunted, retreating as fast as he could. Rather than help with the shopping, he spent the rest of the time sweating in the car.

"Are you ill?" Mrs. Nestler wondered when she found him in the parking lot.

"It's too much," he wheezed.

Mrs. Nestler's face contorted with confusion. "Things might look different, but everything's the same as it's always been," she said, failing to understand that both the world and her son had changed, and that they hadn't changed together.

"Take me back," he pleaded.

***

It was only in his room that Jack felt at ease. He spent days in there, weeks. He kept the door closed, the blinds shut tight, counting off the days as though serving a second sentence.

"I don't understand why he hides," he heard his mother's voice through the wall.

"He's not hiding," Mr. Nestler asserted. "He's living the only way he knows how."

"But what does that mean?"

"It means he's not the boy you or I remember." His voice lowered. "That man in there is not our son…he's a stranger."

***

"Come out here, Jack," Mr. Nestler called the next time Mrs. Nestler was away.

"What is it," Jack, who'd opened his door just a crack, called.

"Your mother's worried."

"What about?"

"You don't come out of that room."

"I don't want to be in the way," he lied.

"You have to get out more. Make your mother happy."

Jack chewed his lower lip and dragged a hand through what little hair was left atop his head. "I'll try," he muttered.

"Tell me something," Mr. Nestler said. "Why'd you have to do it?"

Jack felt himself deflate. "I thought you believed me," he said, his words hollow in his head.

"I said your mother believes you."

"I didn't do it," Jack heard himself say, his words halting.

"Jack," Mr. Nestler said in a tone that Jack hadn't heard him use since he was a very small boy, "there was evidence."

"I didn't do it," he said again.

"People saw you with her."

"I didn't do it." Tears glistened in the corners of his eyes.

"I could forgive you."

"My room..." he said.

"When will you see?"

"I have to go to my room."

Jack fled. Back to his cell. Away from the warden.

***

"How about a movie this afternoon?" Mrs. Nestler asked after breakfast.

"No—" Jack started to say, but his objection was cut short by a stab of his father's eyes. "It's time I found a job," he said. "So that you won't be stuck with me forever."

"We're not stuck with you," his mother assured him. She pulled on his shoulders to give him a kiss on the cheek. "But I know you'll do great out there."

Jack walked with his hands in his pockets, his head low in

front of him to avoid the stares of those nearby. He watched his feet pass over the concrete, unsure of where he was headed or what he'd tell his parents when he returned.

The sound of laughter – innocent laughter – brought his chin up from his chest some time later. To his left there was a playground. On its swings and slides were children no older than eight. Nearest to him was a sandbox full of toddlers constructing temporary towers. When a ball rolled his way, he couldn't ignore the child calling for a little help.

Jack picked up the ball, smiled and heaved the toy across the park while his feet brought him ever closer to the sandbox. It seemed that the toddlers were calling to him too. They were kind, unaware. They wouldn't judge him. He knelt in the sand, his hands gently caressing one of the sculptures.

In his moment of delusion, Jack overlooked the anxious parents huddled on the park's bench. They raced to the sandbox, whispering harsh words and casting unforgiving glares while they swept their children up and raced away, causing Jack to melt into the sand. "I didn't do it," he cried. "I didn't do it!"

Kicking up sand, Jack staggered out of the box and broke into a run.

"I didn't do it," he panted. "I didn't do it...I didn't do it..."

He left the park behind as the children's laughter turned to sobs over their sudden removal. The cries kept up with Jack, chasing him, reminding him of sadness he'd once erased.

He ran through the street screaming and sobbing, his sight blurred by tears, his arms flailing frantically in the air. A cacophony of blaring car horns sounded around him, but he didn't snap out of his moment of madness until screeching tires skidding against the asphalt brought an SUV to a stop right in front of him.

Jack came to a sudden stop as well, aided by the SUV's hood, which he bounced backward off of, nearly falling to the asphalt. Stunned silence, brought on by everyone exhaling their relief, reigned for an incessant second. And then Jack looked up and his eyes locked with those of the man driving the SUV.

The man, his face a twisted scowl, did a double take. His jaw dropped. His forehead smoothed. His complexion went wan.

"You!" he sneered upon leaping out of the SUV. "How dare you show your face around here?"

Jack stumbled backward. His unsettled nerves came together to form a writhing ball of sick in his stomach. He knew the man. He'd seen him before: in court, when the man had pointed Jack out as the one who'd gone off with his daughter.

"I didn't—" Jack started, but his voice failed him.

"You deserve to be dead!"

The man moved forward and then back, advancing on Jack and then retreating, unsure of what his raging emotions would compel him to do. He got back into the SUV and fired it up. Jack thought he'd be flattened for sure. Even so, his paralyzed limbs kept him from fleeing.

Through the glass of the windshield, Jack could see the man's lips moving. What he mouthed was something so foul, so cruel, that it could only have come from a parent who's lost a child in the most vicious of ways. He leaned on his horn, holding the harsh note of condemnation until Jack reclaimed his wits and took off down the street once more.

"Jack, what is it?" Mrs. Nestler inquired when her son came bursting in.

He ran for his room without saying a word, slamming the door shut behind him. But even there, peace didn't come. It was as if there was a swift split in his brain and one side of it was showing him images of something that wasn't possible, yet which suddenly seemed so clear in his mind.

The bed. He saw it for what it was. He saw that something horrible had happened there.

"No!" he screamed, upturning the mattress, which smashed against the wall.

"Jack!" Mr. Nestler hollered outside the door. "What's going on in there?"

Desperate to cover up what he'd done for fear of the price he'd pay, Jack righted the bed just as Mr. Nestler threw open the door.

"What have you done?" the old man wondered.

"Nothing, sir," Jack uttered; only this time he wasn't so sure.

***

Jack seldom left his room after that day in the park. He ventured out only for the bathroom and sometimes to sit at the dinner table, but only at his father's command.

"You're not a prisoner anymore, Jack," Mrs. Nestler would cry outside his room. "Come out. Come out and be free."

But Jack couldn't come out. He couldn't escape his cell and he couldn't ignore the revived visions that showed him things that he himself would have reported to the police.

Sometimes he thought his cage was getting smaller. Sometimes it felt so close around him that he couldn't keep from erupting in fits of claustrophobic and confined rage. On some occasions – when some star of mercy shined upon him – he couldn't remember how he got there. And when that happened he'd often wonder why no one would let him out. But when things got really bad, when Jack felt so squashed that he thought he might suffocate, he found himself clawing at the unbendable bars, which sometimes appeared as locked doors or movable, but impenetrable, chain link surrounding him.

"Jack," Mrs. Nestler squeaked as she set a tray on the floor next to Jack who had his upper body buried beneath the bed, "what are you doing down there?" She peeked around the bed to see what he was working at on the opposite wall. "What are those marks you're making?"

"Nothing," he said, popping out from under his bed. "It's nothing."

Mrs. Nestler recoiled at Jack's appearance. "How'd you get those scratches on your face?" she asked when surely she should have known.

Jack's mouth twitched up from a frown to an unseemly smile, then back to a frown again. No answer came from him. His world was crashing around him. His cell became smaller. In a mad fit of desperate rage, he lunged at his cage, scratching and clawing until more flesh accumulated under his fingernails and blood dripped down his face. He scratched and he clawed, but the cell would not open. The cage would not break.

File #92
JO NEACE KRAUSE

Anniversary

It had been a month since their last visit. She had saved every day to buy the new clothes, but it was worth it. For she looked great, just great. Excitement flushed her cheeks; she took two niacin pills to make them throb. She liked the flushed look, like something wild come out of a slamming wind, and the designer jeans fit so perfectly, just perfect! Everything went so well together, the jeans, the thin white linen blouse through which her bra straps and a small tattooed tiger curled above her left breast were visible. So now she was ready.

Ready for inmate #94312, Sonny Arweed. She felt he was her award for daring to write after seeing his name in the news, and she would be his saving angel against the doom he had fallen into. Of course she could never find anyone like him on the outside; he was the best. Nothing slovenly about Sonny. He made use of the prison library, read law books, was studying Spanish, practicing on the Latino prisoners. She thought of his handsome mouth twisted, trying out the unfamiliar sounds; then she could almost die from wanting to kiss him.

And today was their first anniversary. She had been coming here to the prison for a year now. There was an automatic camera booth in the visitors room where they could have their photographs made and she was thinking about how she and Sonny would stand, smiling and look especially alive on their special day. She would carry the photographs home, evidence of a secret exciting life. She would hang the pictures on her wall where her mother would see them, threatening to tear them up. "You better not tear them up. Sonny said..."

"Sonny's shit, you'll learn that one day," her mother would say, pointing her finger. "You're just another one who's got a lot to learn."

Sonny stood, came along to be photographed, placed himself behind her, legs planted apart like a good actor called up to the stage to do an act, his hand on her shoulder, his dark eyes focused straight ahead into the eye of the camera. The lights flashed. Sonny liked that; he was proud of his looks.

"I look awful!" she cried.

"You look gorgeous!" he contradicted her with that air of superior indifference she knew he cultivated to keep safe, as far back from the world as possible.

"No, I'm hideous!" she persisted, putting her hand up to her hair and laughing. Laughing and teasing. "It's thanks to you, good looking, only to you, that we make such a great picture," she confessed as the finished photographs came rolling wet out of the slot. "It's really so exciting! "she continued. "With you, no visit is ever, ever over; it runs in my mind at home, all night long. Oh, Sonny, I feel so happy just sitting next to you. Do the other prisoners ask you stuff? I mean about me? Talk about us? I bet they do because they all look at me when I come in. Like they just want to see what I have on. The guards give me the once-over too. Maybe I'm becoming a star visitor. I guess because I'm tall. I don't see any other tall women here. Just short ones, girls who look like they've been left out of life. But not us, not us. And you know what? Our conversations never hit a rock, do they?"

"Hit a rock, huh? How about a rock pile?" he laughed in his throat, in his distant mindless way.

"Yes, its amazing how our relationship keeps going," she whispered. "Mom says it's the packages I tote up here to you. The cigarettes and crackers. But she's wrong, its love, this love between us." She bent close against his shoulder and whispered, "For, oh, I do love you even if that love is happening between these walls and that scary barbwire surrounding us, even if we can never meet outside this one crowded room, life with you is still a road that takes wild turns, all of them very adventurous and a cause to puzzle. Which is why I want—I want…will you to tell me more about yourself? Things you've never told anyone but me. Please. Tell me. Why safe cracking? Why did you take to doing box jobs?"

"Well, I'll tell you what I told the judge. I told him I guess I was just sick and tired of having nothing. Working for five dollars an hour when one box job got me twenty-five thousand. One night. Look, honey, maybe to you… to you maybe it is adventurous here," he said. Then as he went silent and hateful, the pleasure drained from her face in shock. "Adventurous to you I guess!" he repeated, "But to me it is a torment, maddening. At times I wish you would not even come down here with your load of wanting. I have never met a woman who wanted love so much and so bad—it's strange... and from a man who cannot give it to her—bad as he wants to give it to her. So it is a goddamn torment to me, a real torment! And I do not want to ever hear again how wonderful it is to come sit at some little shitty stone table, filthy stained with slop, coke spills and cigarette burns, and crap, sit here imagining what it would be like to hold you naked in my arms with your hair down. I want that--my one night with you, naked, your clothes off--like you cannot imagine, Yeah, I want it for real, and it eats at me like a flooded river chews away at its banks. Just one time is all I want. One time. She looked at him, spellbound, dazzled. No one but Sonny could dazzle her like this. The way he was talking, it was real life.

"No," he said. "You know what they called me on the outside? I bet you don't know. One Time Sonny they called me, Thrill a minute, Sonny... because one time is all I ever want from any woman. I didn't care who they are—still don't...it's one time and I'm finished with them. I can't stand the smell of them after that! But now I can't have even that!"

She sat on, taking in these last words, and she was suddenly shocked in a bitter and sudden gloom hearing him say he couldn't stand the smell of a woman after one time. "Maybe you should try a man," she said. "See what that smells like."

"Now... hey, look! Oh, hell, I'm sorry. Looks like I spoiled your day. Ha ha ha. Your face—it's gone down like a blister stuck with a pin," he said, putting his fist over her hand but still not turning towards her. He was glancing over the room. He waved to another prisoner, briefly.

To her it hardly seemed possible that a turn-around could happen so quickly, that he would cut and tear at her like this, so brutally. It was a horrible moment. Her very insides hurt. She could see herself walking out now, see her feet, her high heels transporting her like little stages across the concrete floor, the other prisoners looking as if somehow they knew. Maybe he had told them, bragged to them. "Today I'm going to let her know. Going to give it to her!" She knew only that she had to leave. Yet she sat on with his hand over her own as he looked at the crowd.

A long time ago her school had burned down. Several students burned to death, the bodies were pulled out of the heat and left to cool on the ground. A small dog came up and ran off with a part of one dead girl. A man took a club and killed the dog. She stared for a long time at the hot glowing, collapsing building, the yelping dog, the panting man. The building burned for days. She kept going back, hanging around, staring at it all, just like nothing had happened. The first day when she got home her mother ran to her, weeping... my God, I've been looking all over for you! I've been half crazy calling around. The school on fire ....like the whole world was on fire. And what were you doing down there? Just watching it burn, huh? One of these days, Sara, you might find out how you can burn up too, in a flash. Just keep it up and you'll find out.

"I'll write," she told Sonny.

"You won't," he said.

She didn't answer as she pushed herself away from the table, taking her purse with her. "I'll go up to the canteen room," she said in a low voice.

"You want a coke?"

"Yeah, but if I drink it, I'll just start pissing. Bring me some candy. Couple bars. Snickers."

"Be right back," she said. But she did not come back. She walked in the other direction holding her eyes away from him and towards the tall iron gates which the guard opened for her without looking at her. She wondered how long Sonny would sit at the table waiting, looking down at the floor before he smiled.

From the UV Files

File #96
CASSANDRA DALLETT

850 Bryant

Went to Jail today,
to get a rap sheet
through metal detectors
and elevators out of a 60's Police Show
found the right room
down a long marbled hall
of plexi-glass windows
people shuttling in and out of doors
with numbers on them.

Memories float up from downstairs
of wood paneled courtrooms
where this future was decided
long ago
nerves balanced on folding wood seats
or worse
the holding cell out back
cement seat
cement walls
toilet paper roll for pillow
a slight softness
in a hard box
of back pain and hemorrhoids.

Orange sweats like every other
antsy desperate person
in this funky tight space
smells brown
like wet paper towels.
Wait for your name
eat lunch from a small cardboard box
dry bread a packet of mustard.

From the UV Files

You waited and you waited
no make up or hair brush
a black plastic comb
raw porous you
under fluorescent
ill-fitting orange always looks guilty
in front of the judge
un-cuffed for a minute
the public pretender plays the role
over your shoulder you sneak a look
at the wooden chairs
but see no one
there for you.

Back to the holding cell
the maze of granite behind chambers
echoing with keys and deputy's black shoes.

A future doomed
to return here
some day
even if not in custody.

To go to a little window
on one of these floors
between the cells upstairs
and the courtrooms down
ask for printed numbers
on a page
case numbers
violation numbers
docket numbers
numbers that represent who you were
what you did
and what you are allowed to become
these numbers have followed
you through life.

From the UV Files

Many times
you placed a thumb
rolled it
gave up another
then all of them
slowly rolling
giving up your magnificence
an art display you were born with
your very own map
of future
and past.

From the UV Files

File #99
SARA LETOURNEAU

Naked Truth

"High school teacher charged with possession of child porn"

The headline screams at me,
and so does the teacher's name.
I shake my head, forsaken
by speech but not by thought.
How could they mistake
this gentle, charismatic man I knew
for a pervert?

Memories swarm with questions –
His classroom,
his wire-rimmed glasses
and neatly pressed tie,
how he could wake twenty-seven apathetic minds
with the glint
of a book's hidden treasure.

We grew trees in Brooklyn
and danced in Capulet's ballroom
with him.
We wrote sonnets and found
traces of ourselves in fictional characters
because of him.
He taught me to write without thinking
and to think without wavering –
two morals I still follow.

But, what of his morals?
Was there an impulse behind his smile?
At home, would he find company
in photographs of 12-year-old girls
who were barely flourishing?
Did he find more satisfaction in studying

From the UV Files

his own daughter
than sleeping in the bedspace
next to his wife?

What I thought I knew
and what I wish not to know
have collided – a frontal boundary
of knowledge provoking
a storm in me.
I see its eye, but if I look at it
I have to accept the words I read.
And I must –
it's his final lesson:

No one is ever who they seem to be.

From the UV Files

File #101
CHRISTIAN RILEY

A Place to call Home

At the age of seventeen, Freeda Pill left the country to live in the city. She had visions of standing on stage, living a different life through her lines. She imagined her long legs waltzing down a red carpet through a tornado of smiles, flashes, hairdos, makeup, shoes, martinis and gorgeous people. Freeda had dreams of stardom, but she would have settled for the role of an extra in a Pepsi commercial, because most of all, what she wanted more than anything else was a place of her own.

Freeda wanted to walk through a front door that did not exude the smell of apple pie when opened. She hoped never again to see such gaudy, floral furniture hogging up space in a front room, like some errant, territorial bush that had found its way in through a crack in a wall. Her beautiful blaring eyes, full and green, never again wanted to look at the countless knick-knacks randomly placed onto ledges, mantles, shelves, and tables. Little things that meant nothing, not even to the ones they had been given to, but there all the same, cluttering. Freeda wanted nothing to do with such pieces anymore, because for her, they did mean something. Touch them, if she wanted a scowl. Move them, if she desired dreadful anger. Pick them up and throw them out the window if Freeda wanted seventy-nine lashings from her father's willow branch.

And Freeda longed to be surrounded by barren walls; not ones mounted with the heads and bodies of furry critters, hundreds of eyes staring back at her day and night, crying, pleading, begging for answers: Why? Why am I here, frozen in death, forever doomed to look upon my murderers? Her father's taxidermy business paid well, but not well enough to hire an assistant who could assume Freeda's horrific responsibilities in the garage.

Seventeen-year old Freeda Pill wanted to move through a house that had no pictures in it. Pictures of pale faces, lively for the camera, pretending joy, happy-go-lucky for the sake of the family, the holidays, and look at that man behind the flash, cooing and shaking a fucking teddy bear to a group of adults because they actually thought it was funny and laughed. SNAP! Captured and printed: the fleeting moments of happiness.

Freeda Pill wanted a place to call home.

***

She found an apartment in the South Bronx and cried herself to sleep that first night. She felt lonely, remorse, yet happy as well. She never told her mother or father where she was going. She just disappeared one afternoon, the family savings account from under her parents' mattress stashed into her purse, as she stepped onto the eastbound Greyhound bus.

Her luggage was single, and scarce, containing only essential clothing, and a few pairs of shoes. But this was Freeda's plan. And with a lasting smile, that first week in her apartment she beamed with excitement as she decorated her home with absolutely nothing at all.

Freeda found a waitressing job. And while pouring coffee for strangers, her mind danced circles throughout her apartment. It was a filthy dump, smelled of stale cigarette smoke, cat dander, cat piss, and at best, had unreliable wall-sockets that had already destroyed two hair-dryers. But Freeda didn't care. Her only concern was that since the apartment came "furnished," she needed a way to dispose of the old furniture that did nothing but take up space. And even though she entertained the thought of keeping the kitchen table, Freeda decided against it one morning while eating oatmeal on the window ledge that overlooked the alley below. That same day, she bought a hammer from a local hardware store, smashed all-to-hell her furniture, and tossed the pieces down into the alley through that window.

***

Two weeks later, to her surprise, Freeda felt something. It dawned on her, this "feeling," as she paced her empty apartment one evening, dining on Top Ramen noodles: something seemed to be missing. Freeda bought a plant the next day, and placed it on top of the refrigerator. She smiled, content with this single decoration, hers and hers alone, nothing to it. And Freeda remained content for another week, until she spontaneously bought a book shelf at a thrift store, on her way home from work. Three painstaking hours later, there it stood, finally assembled, against a wall: an empty tower of oak-laminated particleboard. Freeda had a raging tantrum that night, screaming at herself in the bathroom mirror, vowing never again to waste money on such useless items. In the morning, she retrieved her hammer from the kitchen drawer.

But to Freeda's vast disappointment, the feeling that something had been missing from her apartment lingered on, plaguing her mind long after she had stared holes into the barren walls. Like an angry hunger, or insatiable thirst, this feeling swam inside her even as she smashed real holes into those walls with her hammer. And it wasn't until a freak incident occurred—one of criminal intent—before Freeda glimpsed a possible solution to the puzzle of her new home.

***

Mr. Pizza Man broke down with hysterical laughter when he entered Freeda's apartment. She thought him cute, and invited him in while she counted her money.

"Christ! You just move in, or something? This place is a fucking tomb!"

"How much do I owe you?" Freeda asked, her eyes sullen and hurt.

"Well now...that depends on a few things, don't it?" The pizza man's own eyes turned a mood. They became dark, sinister. It all looked too easy for him: a gorgeous brunette, apparently living alone, with nothing at all to protect her and her curvy body from the likes of him.

He placed the pizza down onto the kitchen counter, then unzipped his pants. "How would you like it, sweetie? On your knees, or right up your..."

Although, there was that hammer.

Freeda also had a steak knife, and relying on her experience from her father's business, it took her no time at all to make pieces out of Mr. Pizza Man. In her wisdom, she knew she should have called the police, but again, there was that "glimpse" of a resolve that had struck a chord in her body, like the relief one felt at the end of a very long and loud wail. With each cut of flesh, snap of sinew, and crackle of bone, Freeda believed she was working toward this resolve. And later in the night, as she stood in the middle of her apartment, soaked in blood, chewing on pizza, Freeda smiled and stared at her walls, which were no longer barren, riddled only with holes from her hammer.

Of course, he wasn't the first pizza man to have disappeared in the South Bronx. And when the police came to her door the next day, Freeda made sure she wore nothing but a bath towel, and a country-girl's charm. The officers left her building minutes later, lewd images touring through their minds. Freeda was a good actor, after all.

However, the ensuing days that had passed left Freeda with a sense of doubt. Although she now had "decorations" on her walls, she woke each night in a thrashing fit within her sleeping bag on the floor. That dreaded feeling of incompleteness had crept back into her mind, picking away at her sanity even while she slept. Freeda realized her apartment longed for more than just the pizza man.

***

While watering her plant one morning, she contrived a plan. Men were beasts, slaves to their instinctual cravings that kept them dumb and foolish. Like children to candy, they would follow a beautiful woman home, wherever that may be, as long as the promise of a pair of opened legs were there to greet them. And Freeda's plan, with this assumption about men, worked. Even as these strangers walked into her living room, gasping in disbelief at her hollow apartment, with its walls of "things," they must have thought they had just entered into the Succubus' lair, a fantasy Freeda knew all men had. With their eyes dazzled by a concoction of imagined lust, and the observation of what they now realized were fragments of "human being" mounted on the walls, these men never caught site of the hammer as it struck them furiously in the back of the head. Thus, Freeda endowed her apartment with more decorations.

Weeks went by, with Freeda now being content. Although never cozy, her home became more and more comfortable with each piece of body added to the walls. She thought of this gruesome décor, how it reminded her of her last home. And of this, she thought as well. Did her parents still worry about her? Did they ever? While living there, they seemed only interested in maintaining the charades Freeda had grown up with, no matter what the cost.

Every nook and cranny of that country home harbored some sort of sin upon Freeda's life. Whether in the form of a North American Black Bear that took seconds to kill, yet hours to prepare; or the refrigerator magnet from Hawaii that rewarded Freeda with a violent whipping as a child, after peeling the magnet away. Every nook and cranny stuffed with memories of living, for the living; stuffed with memories of pain, for the child; and stuffed with bodies of the dead, for the dying.

Freeda supposed she had been trying to create something with her apartment. Perhaps in the process of building a new home, she could wipe away the horrors of her last one. A new home meant a new life that meant new memories; memories only for her to create.

Eventually, Freeda realized the flaw in her plan. Like an Interior Designer, she stood in the middle of her apartment, drinking coffee, staring. In the dank corners, where dust and grime had gathered itself long before Freeda had moved in, she saw a scrawny dog chew away at bloody fur, its mind bitten into lunacy by countless fleas. She saw trembling children, hiding in the shadows from a man with a bottle in his hand. From down the hall, in her bedroom, Freeda heard the screams of a woman being beaten by her pimp. And now, looking upon the walls of her own house, staring at the various portions of men she had lured in there, the pieces of their bodies now homeless, robbed of their own "completeness" by the expert hands of a butcher, Freeda finally observed that this wasn't the home she had longed for either. She observed that this home too, had memories of its own.

However, what Freeda failed to observe were the abundant trails of blood that had flowed down those walls. Or, more precisely, where those trails had gathered to, through a collective current due to the misshapen floors of her ancient apartment; a single corner of pooled blood. And while Freeda wrote a letter to her parents, explaining the reasons for her sudden departure, asking for forgiveness yet promising nothing in return, that pool explored the hidden cracks of her apartment, of the building itself, and ultimately, of the apartment below her.

Freeda signed the letter with a simple statement: I think I'm coming home, then looked up after she heard the scream. This time it was a real scream, and not from her bedroom. Thirty feet below, the plump, elderly figure of Mrs. Zimmerman wrestled with her La-Z-Boy, frantic in her attempt to escape from the sticky plasma dripping down into her white hair.

Freeda placed the letter on top of her refrigerator, next to the plant, then entered into a new world stuffed with super-stardom. Her long legs waltzed through a tornado of grim faces, flashing lights, hideous people. No one knew who this girl with the country charm was, every detail about her person a fabricated component leading to nowhere. False identification. Undocumented fingerprints. Strings of incoherent babble coming from her own mouth, offering one dead end after another. And even the letter found in her apartment, written to her supposed parents, was only half complete in that it came without an addressed envelope. When asked about this detail, Freeda drew a blank face and said nothing at all.

***

An asylum upstate took her in. It offered a sprawling view of maple and pine, lush greenery expanding the barred windows of the recreation room. Everyone had a good laugh over her last name, "Pill." Even the faculty thought it ironic, most befitting.

Freeda spent her first three months in silence. Eventually, the patients and orderlies stopped caring about this. And over the next three months, Freeda observed her new "home," with its padded walls, sterile corners, soft bed. She stared at her surroundings, day and night, searching, discovering the wonderful, blank tapestry of a white room. There was nothing to remind her of her past. No memories hiding in the corners, or faces upon the walls, asking, judging.

But then Freeda realized that something seemed to be missing from this new home of hers. Some sort of, "decoration."

It came to her one evening, lying on her bed, staring up at the blank ceiling. Freeda laughed with ironic glee, for on this night she discovered an assortment of magnets, knick-knacks, and other things to scatter around her empty room. And hours later, from a bloody wrist, she added the final touch upon a wall: three words echoed by her bloodstained mouth as she wrote them. "Home at last."

From the UV Files

File #107
BEAU JOHNSON

Resty Acres

In the beginning I didn't believe him; nor would you, all told. The tip off should have been the coffee he brought me.

In the six years I had known Emil Dimpton, he had never given up anything to anyone free of charge. In his infinite wisdom (add sarcasm here), I think he thought that buying me my morning Joe should have made me more inclined to believe his tail of fancy. He'd been wrong, of course, as I have already stated, but only for a while; in the end, but perhaps more so in the middle, I came to believe as much as he. God, I say, should help us all.

My name is Walter Meade and I am seventy-six years old. I am writing this because there needs to be an account of what went on here---what is going on here. As I did not believe Emil there at the beginning, no one has believed it coming from my mouth either. Of this I am sure and why I have chosen to detail it this way instead. No matter. It needs to be noted. It needs to get out. I will write and make copies and send them by mail. It will appear as though I am sick, the conclusions to be drawn unavoidable; that I will seem the senile old fart, sane but for a dementia which lurks. This is the risk I take. This is how scared I am. With what life I have left, I wish to remain.

As you are aware, I am crippled; my light and legs lost to me long ago, each to the same event—the one which took my wife as well as my mobility. I live in this retirement home that someone, some young upstart I've no doubt, decided to call Resty Acres. Some funny, huh? That name. Resty Acres. No, not really. Kind of sad, actually, when you really sit and ponder it. It is a nice enough place, very quiet, very clean, consisting of a menu which still finds ways to surprise me. Also, I have yet to be beaten since my eldest dropped me here some eight years ago. And just so we're clear—I don't hold it against you, Barry, for leaving me here like you did. You are the oldest, the responsibility fell to you. If it were me in your shoes I would have done the same. Not only because I had become a burden, but because you have your own to take care of now. I am old now, yes; what more could one such as me have to offer someone like you? Just because I brought you in this world, fed you and clothed you, nurtured and guided you, ensured you received your schooling—and then your doctoring, what would I deserve in return? Nothing. As you've given, son—as you've given. I wish you well, boy. As I do your brothers and sisters.

Pricks. The lot of you. Am I bitter? Little bit.

Back to it, then.

It was a Tuesday when Emil came to me with the free cup of Joe. And right from the get go you could tell that something was off, that the man was struggling; some unseen weight seemed to be pulling at his corners, the ones which keep the majority of us in check. For an old codger awaiting his last day, he was an unusually upbeat fellow is what I mean to say; but he was far from that on this particular day. No, on this day Emil was scared. I would go so far as to say terrified even. His color was off as well, his face almost ashen except for these dark circles which hung beneath his eyes like used tea bags—the round kind, not the square. He kept wiping his head too, with that damn handkerchief of his, which would have been much weirder if the old boy still had hair. Slowly, he explained what had happened as best he could. Done, he pleaded with me to believe him, that he didn't think anyone one else would. I agreed with him, as it was poppycock, what he told me, but balderdash was the word I think I used to explain it to him.

"But Walter, it took Vera! I don't want to be next."

"And you won't be," I said, more than a little patronizingly. "Emil, if what you say is true, then size will prove your friend. It makes you too big for it to take you. Besides, how do you know Vera hasn't had one of her episodes and only went wandering, as she's been known to do? You don't. Therefore until she turns up, you cannot know. Not for sure."

He looked at me then, and I could tell his confusion remained, thicker now than when he first sat down. This had not been my intent.

Around and around his handkerchief went, damn thing—wiping whatever it needed to wipe. "But I am losing weight every week, Walter. I am only above one hundred and twenty as of this morning. I am very close to the pattern weight, I think."

"Emil, seriously, we are too old to believe in things such as these. There are no vampires, especially ones which eat entire victims. When have you ever heard of a vampire doing that? How would it be possible even? Is it not only for the jugular, the drinking of and what not?"

"Do not patronize me, Walter." And there was real anger there, a flash of it anyway. "Three of us have gone missing in the last two years, four now with Vera. All unaccounted for. Off wandering they say, always in the middle of the night, all of it conveniently blamed on senility, of course. Do you think I have not thought this through? Do you not think I have seen?"

"Emil, you yourself said it was dark when you saw and that you couldn't really see."

"But the noises I heard."

"Yes. But hadn't those awakened you? Is it possib—

But it was too late. He was up and gone without so much as a glance back towards me, that damn handkerchief searching for something, searching as always. It was only later that I realized I hadn't even popped the lid to the coffee Emil had tried to bribe me with. I'm sure if some shrink thought hard enough they would be able to form some sort of correlation between this and what was about to happen.

Yes, quite sure.

**

I didn't see Emil much after that morning and the times that I did, he didn't look much better than when he first told me about the vampire he believed was hidden amongst the elderly here at Resty Acres; his appearance seemed to be on the decline, deteriorating little by little each time I saw him in the weeks which followed. I don't know exactly when it happened, but there actually came a time when he chose to no longer dress himself. Moreover, his hygiene was beginning to suffer as well. Ultimately, he ended up wearing nothing more than underpants and that housecoat of his, the one with black stripes. He still had his handkerchief, however, that same old red one, although it seemed to be getting less and less work the more times I saw him; mostly I would see it dangling from his hand, limp as his new demeanour. It was when Emil himself went missing that things began to change for me.

Or rearrange, if I am to be truthful.

When Emil and I had the talk that Tuesday morning, I was given new perspective.

I am very close to the pattern weight, I think.

That is what he said, there at our table in the breakfast room. Odd, yes, but as I think back over the times I saw him wandering to and fro in that housecoat of his, it occurs to me that Emil did seem to be on the decline in weight as well. The man was becoming less is what I mean to say, smaller and thinner each time I took notice I suppose. Still, thinking back, maybe I could have prevented some of this; maybe, maybe not. At least I could have put forth an effort, which is something I did not do, not then. And of this I am ashamed, just so you know, as it places my character beneath a light I am unfamiliar with.

Before all that, however, I received my new roommate. His name was Stanley Chesterfield, and if that name isn't a handle then I don't know what is. I called him Flat Stan on account of his face, which really needs no further explanation. He was a smaller man, and frail, from years of bed rest I'm sure. He was also uncommunicative. Not totally, but unable to hold a conversation concerning the here, the present and the now. Poor Flat Stan had come to be my roomy while he found himself trapped within the end stages of Alzheimers. This prison, Alzheimers, is a disease no one would wish upon their worst enemy. It is rampant here at Resty Acres, perhaps the disease du jour, and believe you me when I say it is as powerful as it is heart-wrenching. A fear of mine I'll admit, but no longer my number one. No, that place is now reserved for the impossible proved possible, for the stuff I used to know as make believe.

I have looked evil in the eye, my friend. I am afraid to say it does not blink.

**

A meeting was called concerning Emil's disappearance, the entire residence escorted into the auditorium before lunch, three days after the search had been called off. The smell was there, of course, as it always is. And don't think we are immune, because we aren't. We know it's there, hanging over and rising from us like an invisible prophet. The death smell is what I'm referring to, the yellow smell of the elderly, of chemical and approaching death. In a room such as ours, with over two hundred seniors... well...you get the drift---no pun intended.

Dr. Hamilton is the guy who runs the show here, the Big Tuna as it were, and has done so since before my children decided me a member. He's a slick one, is Dr. Hamilton, him and that new-age ponytail of his. I didn't always know he was this slick, and only came to after this meeting. Oh yes. Indeed. It was when he started in on how Emil had been battling what I had previously called the disease du jour that I really began to see the situation for what it was: a railroad, as in we were being.

Emil Dimpton never had any such disease. This is true. This I know.

We were then informed that stronger security measures would be in place by week's end. This in light of the "now recurring" and "very unfortunate" theme which had found its way into the "very heart" of Resty Acres itself; that with Emil's disappearance as well as Vera's, lest we forget Hickman and Robalard, (whom he did not mention by name, just so we are clear) that the board had gathered—in the eleventh hour, I'm sure—and voted unanimously on a new mandate, one which was to be "swift" and "immediate" in its "execution" and "implementation." Ah. How nice. They care! They really, really care.

What I said was this: "Dr. Hamilton?"

"Walter, yes, you have a question?" Not Mr. Meade. Walter. There you go.

"Yes," I said and paused, momentarily wishing for the deadwood to work once more. I wanted to stand as I said my piece is all. No reason why, just did; just something which happens to me from time to time. Mostly I'm good with what my situation is, having come to terms with it moons ago, but still, as I've said...it happens...momentary lapses.

"I have known Emil for six years," I continued. "In that time I have never seen any of the symptoms you associate with Alzheimers. How could this be? Are you sure is what I'm asking?"

I half expected to see something register in Hamilton's eyes at this, a darting flash of guilt perhaps, some glaring sheen of hate. What I received was something quite the opposite. Squatting to his knees, the man offered me a tenderness I was up until that point unaware he possessed. He said, "Walter. He was someone you probably saw on a regular basis, was he not? Your friend, maybe? This never makes us the best judges, on our best days. I am a trained physician and Alzheimers the field I specialize in. I would know. Emil was suffering. Silently. And it was coming on fast towards the end, before he went missing. It comes to no surprise that many of you failed to notice." And the slick bastard had me, honestly; hook, line and ponytail. It was when he threw in the wink, there at the end, that two things became very clear, very fast. One was that it had always been an inside job, just as Emil had suspected from the get go. Two was that I had just made myself a target.

**

Now...it's not like any overt changes occurred once Dr. Hamilton let me in on the little secret Emil had been silenced for. No long looks from across the room when I saw him in one of the lounges or many of the hallways or anything like that. Neither was there hissing or the producing of fangs, just so you know. Everything remained as it was before the latest disappearances. Resty Acres reverting back to what it has always been—a retirement home, the kind which serves jell-o after each and every meal.

I was neither hounded nor touched is what I mean to say. Even though I now knew, and knew that Dr. Hamilton knew I knew, I remained alive. And don't get me wrong, I do not know for certain that Dr. Hamilton is the vampire Emil spoke of, only that he is part of the conspiracy residing here.

Days passed, weeks. And as most of you know I tried to get you word, calling as many of you as I could. Do you remember that, Barry? Do your brothers and sisters? How do you recall the times I called and tried to convince you of the plight I faced? What did they tell you when you called back to inquire about the state of your father's mental health? What I think they told you; what I believe they tell all who inquire about the darkness which goes on here; do they apologize and tell you it is senility setting in? Perhaps a bit of the early Alzheimers even? We'll do some tests though, yes, yes, a batch of them, and get back to you with the results. Did it go a little something like that, Barry? I'm pretty sure it did.

Do you see how slick this makes them?

Do you?

From the UV Files

**

Human beings are complex individuals. This has been said before. We are also simple, and at times stupidly so. Like many of us, not much scares me anymore. Some things yes, like disease and war, but none of it gutting me as completely as it had when I was a boy.

I am an abrupt talker and always have been, loud with opinions. It tends to lead people to believe I am cantankerous by nature, and an arse-hole by choice. I am not, however, but far too old and much too tired to explain it away in the document before you. If my wife were alive she would verify the things I have just mentioned. My kids? Not so much. And that is their choice. It was always my way or the highway beneath the roof I built and placed above their heads. I was a stern parent—the need for them to know and understand the very top of our list. This is all I will say about that. They know their bed and how they must lie. What I must get back to is the fear I mentioned earlier, the stuff from my childhood. It is back inside me now, a thing come home to roost. Unwilling to relent, it screams for release.

I have seen the creature at work. As Emil Dimpton believed, it does do more than drink.

**

I had gotten used to Flat Stan's snoring. Not that I had much choice in the matter—he slept most of the time. When he did wake we would talk about the old days, when the grass was greener and all that jazz. During these conversations I was usually somebody else, a Johnny or Duncan, sometimes a David. This didn't bother me, and poor Flat Stan never knew the difference. I think he did come close to the surface once, as there was a pause and then the question of how I ended up in the wheelchair. When I began to tell him my story he asked me what I was talking about and if I thought mother would approve. At this I was back to being Duncan, the older of his two sons. This was how my relationship played with Flat Stan—two parts sleep, one part conversational window into his past. Realizing this forces me to acknowledge that Alzheimers is not unlike the creature which stalks me, that both are draining forces of utter destruction, time and method the only differences I can find between them.

The very night I came to this realization is when the vampire awakened me—overrode the snores I had adapted myself to. Rising towards consciousness I came to know of the sucking sounds Emil had spoken of months ago, the ones which now replaced Flat Stan's exhalations. Poor Flat Stan—there would be no more stories concerning Johnny or Duncan and sometimes a David; I am certain the man was dead before I turned on my reading lamp. In doing so I bore witness to the thing I am writing about, to that which has been preying upon us here at Resty Acres. I can't say for sure that it is a vampire, not in the truest sense of what I know. What I can say is that it shares a lot of the same characteristics I have been shown in movies and TV. Not all, but some. Other things reminded me of leeches, similar to the ones I used to fish with.

Big is unable to do it justice. The thing was massive, six five from head to boot. It was wide as well, as wide as it was thick it seemed. Bent over, its mouth and chin were buried deep into the middle of Stan's chest as it drank, the throat of it bulging to the point of where I thought it might burst. You would consider me turning on the light and sitting up would have made it notice me, yes? Would think I'd be screaming my fool head off for help, no? Both of these things should have happened but neither of them did. I watched if hypnotized, stared as the vampire ex-sanguinated my roommate completely, listened as it sucked and sucked and sucked. It was only when the draining was complete that it turned to me, then and not a moment before. I remained silent as it regarded me, lost within the caverns of the eyes before me. They were black like oil, those eyes, black like death; nothing of white at all. It moved towards me, touched me: a finger to my paunch. "Too much meat," it said, and the words were wet—still coated, swimming in the blood which used to run Stan. This was when my bladder let go, or when I believe it let go. I can't say for sure, not then, not now. After this it turned from me, its attention back to Stan—of what remained of Stan. Standing over him it opened and closed its mouth, a tocking sound accompanying this. At the time I did not know it was flexing. Now, however, I do. It was readying itself, you see; ensuring the route was able.

Slowly at first, then faster, its mouth began to expand, widening to receive another set of fangs, ones which erupted first from the upper part top of its jaw and then from the lower. As was the creature, massive were the teeth that came: large and long and sling blade sharp.

You realize, of course, that the drinking was done?

Okay. To the hole then, back into it; as this is where it went. Slowly it leaned down and re-entered the open cavity of Stan's chest. I watched as it latched on and I watched as I heard it create a seal between its mouth and Stan's wound. After this there came another sound, this one louder than the first, the one it had been making with its jaw. It was deeper too, coming from the breast bone it was making its way through. Once it did this, once it broke through, this is when I truly understood what Emil was trying to convince me of that morning in the breakfast room, the day in which I patronized him more than a little bit.

I am very close to the pattern weight, I think.

I am only above one hundred twenty as of this morning.

I think it can only consume around that much each time, roughly a hundred pounds a pull—its maximum, give or take. Amazing, no? A vampire who does it all. No fuss, no muss, no mess, no body. This is why it chooses the elderly, I think. Not only because we are probably the easiest of prey but because of the practicality we represent; that most of us are already the size it might require, each of us the lightest of light snacks.

The organs were next, all of them, and then the bones, followed, of course, by skin. All of it going, gone, and into it as it continued to feed. Stan's body receding or deflating as it was depleted, everything being pulled up and into the supernatural vacuum it was attached to. Its throat was so engorged with the pressure it was creating that again I had the sense its neck was close to bursting. And I don't know how... but I must have missed something, even though I witnessed it all. It did not chew is what I mean to tell you. Not once. I do not know if it expelled some sort of compound as they were linked—if this is what helped to liquefy what remained of Stan, because, as I've said, there was not an ounce of chewing that went on that night, none; and human bones, last time I checked, were still as hard as they ever were. It seems a logical assumption, no? That it might produce and secrete a toxin to help with what it devours? I know, I know. Where is the logic in any of this? Quite a quandary I've found myself, yes? Yes. Yes, it is.

I am more worried about what it said to me as it left, however, when it turned back from the door to my room once it was ready to leave. Soon was what it said to me; one word, nothing more. It was later that I noticed Stan's bed sheets: that even they did not remain. Taken or ingested I cannot say for sure.

**

That was four months ago. In the time between then and as I write this, many things occurred. The police were called for one, and more than once at that. After the third time I was dismissed with prejudice, informed I would be charged if another instance arose. I told this officer to shove it where the sun didn't shine and that if he felt so inclined then he should go ahead and do it, my pension would hold. Upon reflection I realize this was wrong and ill-advised at best. I was doing exactly what I am trying to warn you about: that no one will believe and the more that I protest the more I seem unstable. Unstable leads to other words here at Resty Acres, words which begin with capitals. I have none of these impairments, however, and of that you can be sure; my faculties are intact, in tune, without a touch. But this is protesting, is it not? Fine. About it I will say no more. Instead I will tell you that I'm scared, that my fear remains.

Too much meat.

That is what it said to me, there in the room I shared with Stan. I know now it was referring to my weight, of the extra amount I had there. When you are suddenly paralyzed it is hard to maintain your previous body weight. Let no one tell you different. It seems you are only eating for half a body, and effectively you are, but the amount you had been used to, that doesn't go away—never has for me, anyway. What I am trying to get across is that everything I ate seemed to fall and hold to the centre of my being once my spine had been severed. The distribution lines breaking down somewhere along the way—the same line my spine had run upon, perhaps. Bottom line: I had a paunch, the creature touched it. At the time it did this I was roughly one hundred ninety pounds. It is not this I worry about, not anymore. That I have dipped below one hundred and twenty as of this morning is what does—Emil-weight if you remember, on the day he brought me coffee. This is what terrifies me. Because I am unable to stop what is happening—that I have been stripped of a basic control. The creature did something to me, must have. Dr. Hamilton would disagree, I'm told, and has expressed as much. He thinks that what I'm doing is to be commended, that it can do nothing but prolong what he already sees as a long, full life. To his credit he kept a straight face. Have I informed you of how slick this man is? Yes, I believe I have. He is not the vampire, though, as I think I have also mentioned. He is only a facilitator. Perhaps a disciple even. Resty Acres, the place he chooses to worship. I don't know, will probably never know. Can only hope I will not die as the others have died and remain uneaten. Tomorrow I will try again, after I have made copies and secured them to the mail. I will need a key, however, and that is where you come in. Can you secure it? Moreover, will you? All the guards have one—it hangs from their shirts. They are new, these keys, no longer metal but instead made from plastic, each of them rectangular in shape.

New security measures; this is what they said.

Too much meat.

Immediate and swift in implementation and execution. This is what they did.

I am very close to the pattern weight, I think.

I can see now what they've done. Can you? They have locked us in here with it, isolating its prey. We are boxed in, all of us, the lid done closed and the sides taped shut. Better yet, you could even say we are now its jell-o, the menu always red. It drinks us and then eats us and no one lifts a finger, not even with me screaming for any who would hear. As I have said before—this is how slick they are, how cunning and keen, running it all out in front there, just below our noses.

For the record, I hope I am loud when it comes. If I know anything about myself, I imagine I will prove to be. That is all one can ask for in this type of situation, I suppose; that in my dying I might (as Emil did for me) wake and enlighten another as to what is really going on here. Perhaps in doing so, he or she will then take up the fight as I took up the fight.

Unlike me, perhaps even he or she might prevail.

From the UV Files

File #118
JONATHAN HINE

Dead Echoes

when I was 21
my life was at a critical juncture
I was a leaf caught in the violent winds of spirit
as fierce riptides of madness pulled me further
and further away from consensual REALITY
too weak & feeble to guide myself
I languished in government housing projects
half starved & half mad
going through what I would describe as
relentless cycles of retribution
my lit third eye or bio-electric/subtle energy sensor
was receiving scrambled & remote astral signals/transmissions
superimposed with the dissonance of personal delusions &
hallucinations
creating a harsh intensity that demanded onward motion
towards some kind of release as
the atmosphere grew heavy
with sighs & distant whispers
every shadow teemed with fleeting specters that
dissipated when I focused on them
all the atoms in the apartment oscillated
according to the hellish harmony of the environment
the walls were thin & noise easily penetrated
from adjacent apartments
the concrete hallway's acoustics reflected
every infernal sound right to my door
the soundtrack of my own personal hell
had all the agonized and furious howling
of madness & despondency
distressed screams of children
would echo from the apartment at the end of the hall
the way the child screamed it sounded as if
someone was putting her hand to a hot stove
at night a hollow sigh would wake me from dreams

From the UV Files

fertile with private terror
the only light in the room
was the hall light
shining through the two inch divide
from the door to the floor
and there was a dark shadow
obstructing the light
DEAD CENTER
on the other side of the door
like someone was standing RIGHT THERE
most of the time I just lay there trying to
figure out what could be casting that shadow
but I when I had to take a piss
I had to face it and would throw open the door
and nothing was there
I would pass out again, awaken & it was gone
just the gleaming two inches of vacant air
and then a few hours later the shadow was back
this went on night after night
until I rolled up an old towel & wedged it
in the crack between the door and the floor
problem solved
until the phenomena morphed into another comparably
bothersome form:
something was playing with the thermostat
I would come home from work in July & the dial on the thermostat
was on the highest setting
the place roasting and reeking from the morning's garbage
I would turn the thermostat off
run the garbage to the dumpster, & open the windows
I always locked my door
& I always checked
the thermostat before I left for work
only to return home to the apartment
sweltering at 110 degrees
and the weirdness continued
one night I returned from a funeral
it was hot so I slept on the foldout couch
with the patio door open

From the UV Files

curtains blowing in the wind
the ominous atmosphere
was charged with a static energy
that crackled & sizzled in the air
I awoke to see a dark & solid figure with his back toward me
he walked into the kitchen
startled, I jumped up & followed him around the corner
but no one was there and that was the only door to the kitchen
before I could get to the bedroom the door slammed shut HARD
right in my face
no one in the bedroom
by a certain implication
these experiences have shown me hints of something
far more deeply interfused
and in spite of everything
I survived those dark days
wounded & undermined
but still alive

From the UV Files

File #121
TIMOTHY BEARLY

The Tragedy of Dick Ellingsworth

By around the year 3030, cryonics—although still fledgling—had become a practical application. No longer merely a topic for science fiction, we now had the ability to preserve humans and their biological systems at low temperature—with the expectation that a particular ailment could be remedied in the future. Unfortunately, not unlike other fields of cutting edge technology, there were only a select few who could afford it. Indeed only the upper echelons, only the uber-rich plutocrats, were awarded this life prolonging service.

Although the manipulation of the human genome and genetic engineering—which had been going on for well over a century—helped to eradicate many diseases that were once thought incurable, viral evolution, namely the evolution of particular RNA viruses, still made certain conditions difficult to treat. Consequently, some—like the affluent philanderer Dick Ellingsworth—saw cryonics as a viable alternative.

Dick was your archetypical greed-is-good, laissez-faire, unbridled free market adherent. He was a kind of guy easily satirized as a rotund schlep with man boobs (C-cup), who falls asleep with Machiavelli's *The Prince* by his bedside, right before wanking off to the picture of Ayn Rand—in the inside jacket cover of The Virtue of Selfishness. The only thing more massive than this behemoth of lard was his inflated ego. Proportional to that was his 10,000 square foot mansion and a net worth somewhere around 500 million. Notwithstanding his inherited trust fund, he insisted that his fortune was obtained through hard work and perseverance— an all too familiar semblance purported by members of the privileged class.

A staunch advocate of Social Darwinism, Dick scoffed at safety net legislation and the concept of the welfare state, which to him was resulting in indolence and "the degeneration of the human race."

"Just as nature culls the herd and weeds out its manifestly inferior organisms, so too should the human race, yet we spend countless tax dollars on the 'less fortunate' only to insure the perpetuation of the contamination of our gene pool," Dick contended. Fortunately the sentiment was only shared by a small faction of well-to-do partisans, innocuous blowhards and fortunate sons. Most of whom would be obliterated wholesale–like defenseless bacterium, in a pool impregnated with chlorine–if ours was a society in accordance with natural selection.

In the realm of politics, what one says in public and what one does in private is seldom harmonic. Dick Ellingsworth epitomized this phenomenon of hypocrisy. He was a latent homosexual who condemned homosexuality. He talked incessantly about strong work ethics, although he never really had to work a day in his life. He championed family values, though he had been divorced three times. And what he said fervently about the concept of "survival of the fittest" apparently did not apply to him—unless of course it is amended as "survival of the fattest." Moreover, when Dick was told that he had just three months to live—because of his congenital inability to fight the RNA virus that infected him—he was not about to let natural selection run its course.

Yep, Dick had the means to access the best health care in the world, but even the best medical equipment and personnel couldn't save him. And after months and months of ineffective treatment, doctors informed him of the high probability that a cure would be found in the next few decades. So Dick eventually opted for cryopreservation.

A month later the medical procedure was set to begin. "I hope you're all republicans," Dick said in jest to the doctors hovering over him—a subtle reference to his beloved "Dutch" icon. Dick loved Reagan, he had a 24x36 painting of the former president in his living room—in which he was added as a fifth face carved into Mount Rushmore.

"Is this going to hurt?"

"Don't worry Dick, you will be given some general anesthetic drugs, fade to black and wake up in a few decades when we can better treat your condition.

"Last words?"

"Excuse me," said Dick.

"Well, we assure you that cryonics is relatively safe, but it is not without risk; a small percentage of our patients are unable to be effectively revived. The mind uploading process is the tricky part;

some subjects seem to respond better to it than others. Cognitive impairment is also a concern, some of our patients awaken in a state of severe catatonia. The risk is minimal, but just in case things go wrong, we ask that all of our clients offer their last words."

"All I can say is that, after I am thawed out, I hope that the state I wake up in is not a welfare state," Dick Quipped.

The medical personnel all responded with laughter.

"Good one sir."

Dick was accustomed to amens and kudos, even more so among his own staff. They seem to have more of a propensity to laugh at your jokes when you can easily fire them on a whim if they don't.

"Ok Mr. Ellingsworth, we are ready to proceed."

Dick took one last look at a photo of himself—a picture of him posing with a rifle—atop a moose carcass that he had found on the side of the road, a suitable metaphor for how he feigns responsibility for his immense wealth. He then gently pressed his lips to the rosary that was given to him by his father—along with the quarter billion dollar estate.

"Ok, I'm ready."

"Now, we need you to count down from ten," the doctor said in a soft voice.

"Ten...nine...eight...seven," and Dick went limp.

II

"Mr. Ellingsworth."

"Can you hear me?"

"Can you hear me Dick?"

Dick's mouth began quivering and his eyelids started to flutter. He began whispering inaudibly, as though he was speaking in tongues.

"I hope we don't have another episode of glossolalia," said the nurse.

Shut up and get me a dose of ammonium carbonate," the doctor responded.

"Mr. Ellingsworth?"

Dick eyes finally stopped fluttering and slowly opened. "Wha...? What happened?" Dick muttered in a hoarse voice.

"Where is the other doctor?"

"Don't worry Mr. Ellingsworth, everything is fine, we are going to get you taken care of."

Unbeknownst to Dick, it was now 3067. He had been hibernating in a Liquid nitrogen cacoon for thirty-seven years, and the world that awaited him was far different from the world he had previously known.

Upon finding out that he had proverbially traveled in time, the first thing he wanted to know was what the political climate was. He didn't waste any time.

"Who is in control of the house and senate?" Dick asked.

"A relatively new party called the Spartiate Caste took control of both the house and the senate about 10 years ago. They have been in control ever since."

After seizing power the fringe right members of the SC immediately began creating new legislation that would help to 'rid mankind of its parasites.' The Eugenics act of 3058 was just one of many such laws."

"Sounds good, it sounds like our nation finally toughened up," Dick responded.

"Interesting to hear you say that," the doctor said under his breath.

"What was that?"

"Never mind, Mr. Ellingsworth."

The Doctor then informed Dick that he was going to be transferred to another facility. After Dick voiced concern, he was subsequently told that he need not worry, and that the medical personnel at the new location would be better equipped to treat him. Two weeks later, after he was fully recovered from being frozen for almost 4 decades, Dick was on a tram headed to a hospital in the east called The Buchenwald Medical Center.

Buchenwald was an immense 13 story medical facility that looked much more like a military compound than a hospital. Surrounding the fortress-like amalgam of buildings was a twenty foot stone wall with barbed wire. Dick began to wonder if he really was being taken to a hospital after all.

"What's with the heavily fortified gate at the entrance?" Dick asked a guard as they pulled in.

The guard then pointed to a sign on the front gate which read: "Keeping our patients safe is our number one priority."

"Safe from what?" Dick wondered.

III

After keeping Dick waiting for hours, a nurse finally escorted him to a dimly lit, enormous, concrete room. Were he not in a hospital he might have thought that he had just stepped inside of a gas chamber.

"The Doctor will be with you momentarily," said the nurse.

"Thanks sugar lips," replied Dick.

Dick often made pathetic attempts to sweet talk the ladies, particularly the young ones, who would have otherwise been out of his league—had he not been rich. But because he had lots of money, he was used to it reciprocating, at least as a pretense. That's why he was taken aback when the young nurse told him, "Go fuck yourself fatass. You have more chins than a thousand year old redwood has tree-rings."

This type of treatment was completely foreign to Dick; he wasn't going to let that little cunt get away with it. Just as he was about to chase her down, to teach her a lesson, the doctor walked in.

"Well Mr. Ellingsworth, according to your DNA results, you have a predisposition for obesity, heart disease and a number of other various diseases. Your life expectancy is approximately 52 years."

"Yeah, and at 57, I think it's safe to say that I have defied the odds," Dick responded. "The good lord has blessed me," he followed up.

"Well, I don't think that the flying spaghetti monster has anything to do with it. You have been kept alive because you were able to receive the medical care that others could not. You have been kept alive because you have had two open heart surgeries. You have been kept alive because you could afford the ten million dollar cryonic procedure. No need to invoke metaphysical, fairy tale creatures here."

Dick was furious. "Nobody talks to me like that," he said, right before he was interrupted again.

"Besides if God wanted to bless you, don't you think he would have just eliminated certain vulnerabilities from your genetic structure, so you didn't have heart disease in the first place?

Because, according to the court ruling, your God appears to have cursed you."

Dick was confused. Why was he, for the first time in his life, being treated like a second class citizen? Though incognizant of the fact, he was now being treated the same way that he had treated others his entire life. Because now he was living in a world where individuals are not assessed and quantified by their FICO score.

"Court ruling? What on earth are you talking about?" Dick responded with ire.

"I am sorry Mr. Ellingsworth, but the ministry of eugenics now has jurisdiction over all medical cases that come in and out of this facility. All citizens are brought before the tribunal to see if they are deemed 'worthy of life.' Unfortunately, in your case, the consensus was unanimously, 'nay.'

"What the... I never went before any court, what kind of system is this?"

"And what would your defense be? DNA does not lie? That is what was brought before the court, your DNA. That is all the evidence they need to determine a subject's value to society. After all, we don't want to be taking care of any societal parasites. Wouldn't you agree?"

Dick was finally living in a "survival of the fittest" utopian society. The kind of society that operated in complete congruency with the law of natural selection. The kind of society where the feeble—less fit—specimens are rooted out. The kind of society where the strongest organisms prevail and assert their will on their weaker counterparts. The kind of society he had ostensibly dreamed of living in. But this megalomaniac's idea—of a darwinian shangri la—was predicated on one important misconception, a delusion of grandeur: the perennial fallacy that those who possess the greatest amount of wealth are those who are the most fit.

From the UV Files

File #127
T.T. JAX

Suck

The baby needs me.

They found her, maybe, or she was born of me in a dream. Somehow through wish and wire she has sewed herself a baby-face; she breathes. She lives here, at Kid Kare, in the Palm Breeze shopping mall where I work.

Kid Kare has a door that leads directly to the beach. Often I take her by the water to a cold cement picnic table. I breastfeed her, although I don't think she has a stomach or can swallow. Sea gulls circle, chill damp wind blows sand into my eyes. She likes the sound of it, the surf—water like a body gone solid wet-whacking the ground, rolling back in tentacles of erosion. It reminds her, maybe, of a womb or guts she's wished for. It sprays us sometimes, a feeling somewhat like being spit on, but by accident, the spitter familiar to us, maybe even loved.

She is an anomaly.

When she is angry, or happy, or in need she can change herself. I don't mean diapers—I don't think she has diapers; perhaps she must. Perhaps I change them. But I mean her face, her body: She can change.

When she is angry she has a face like a sock monkey, but garishly-colored, more bulldog than monkey. Sometimes when she is very angry, she can become something else, or vanish altogether. Once she became a pile of lint in my arms.

She has an eye, though, that is very pink and pretty. When she is happy she hides the angry colors of her face in a bonnet sewn to her neck, and coyly watches from the corner of the one pretty eye. It must be on the side of her head, lidded or retractable; only she can reveal it. She looks more lamb than bulldog then, shy and wishing to be wooed.

Her body feels as one might expect: a slug, a sack of wet rice or perhaps thick pudding. She is not wet—surprisingly warm, dry—but her bonelessness suggests wet things.

Even so she breathes, and even has a little heartbeat, although it is irregular.

I came for her, or brought her; I don't remember. There are others here, human babies with skin and bowels, but I am exclusively assigned to her, like a mother. I don't know where she goes when I leave. Sometimes my co-workers help me find her when she turns to dust, or a bit of frayed yarn that blows away down the beach.

The press has come several times to witness and pry. I don't know how they know about her, but she is known, well-known, even internationally: a living baby doll, a morphing infant unborn. The store front of Kid Kare is plate glass, like a pet store's; all the children and cribs and scattered toys are visible to passer-bys, bright and eerily flat under fluorescent lights. But we shield her from sight. I wait with her in the changing room, behind dark shower curtains hung by a sagging string, whisper her to quiet. They ask many things, but we have no answers to give, other than that we wonder and endure.

I am so tired, drained by her peevishness and the dry hungry suck of her mouth that is, after all, only a little threadbare fold. Sometimes I am reminded why I come here, care for her; mostly I forget. I do believe I love her. Perhaps she is mine, or was. Perhaps I denied her, deprived her of suck and love and left and so she picked up her own pieces, patchworked herself with string in place of sinew; now she calls me, she calls me.

"All I wanted was a puppy," I told a co-worker, as I swung her squalling in firm arms. He watched sideways as I pulled out my breast, wet the cotton of her mouth with milk, slow-spurting and steady. She studied me sleepily with her pink eye; I breathed low to relax, sitting as calmly as I could in a hard plastic chair.

"How do I even know to do this, Brandon? All I wanted was a puppy."

He gently stroked the slow curve of her cheek, round the piping of her mouth, knelt to watch my face. He listens, which is unique among his kind, and he wants to sleep with me, which is less so. Mostly it wearies me, the thought of spreading for him, but I think it. The milk comes faster. Maybe riding him instead, somnambulist rolling hips—or letting him do it as I nap, a bit of drool tender and slow trailing from sleep-slack lips.

I have a boyfriend; his name escapes me although sometimes I remember it by a particular whine or turn of wind as I walk her on the beach. I'm sure I remember when I am home, where he lives. I can see him shaving, a trail of blood-beads perfect like a necklace down his cheek, a sink-full of pinked foam. Perhaps he gave her to me. He says he is proud. I wonder if he would understand if I brought Brandon behind the curtains, just to separate my body skin and sensate from her cotton-stitching cling. I am sure that he has never held her, but he must have heard.

I have a supervisor who is also my assistant, Brad: we are a team, as she is the kind of baby that, left to one person alone, would certainly be dumped in the rubbish. Sometimes I look at her and think: I need new socks. She must sense this—by this point she has memorized the terrain of my palms, surely notes the subtle shifts and clogs of my nostrils, tracks the slack and taut of my forearms as I lift her lumpy to the sky. Because when I look at her, when I see with want the silver flash of scissors, fantasize about the delicious rip of seams yielding to a steady pull, she shows me her pink eye, sweet and deep and calm as a jewel.

In her eye I am a monster, fully reflected, hungry and mean; she loves me, craves me, despite my hostility. I am forgiven, then, seen by her unlike any other. I can do this, I think then, whatever this is, I must. I hold her to me. She is wretched, an anomaly, but perhaps I am, too. A mirror, a test. I lift her mouth to my breast.

Perhaps she belongs to Brad. He is an earnest man, a listener, like Brandon: he understands the close relationship between selflessness and homicide. We won a peace prize—an international peace prize—for caring for her, or perhaps more directly for not killing her. Or maybe it is because she is some reflection of us, something awful we've done to someone else or many others. Maybe she is our hate, helpless and suckling, and our nurturing of her is like a collective wish for forgiveness.

But whatever it is they gave us a prize, only we could not let anyone see how ugly she is, her flat and fuchsia bulldog face, the fierce orange piping of her cheeks, the clamorous lime green of her sewed-on eyebrows—they would be, frankly, horrified. And maybe they should be. Maybe we all should be. But if she can see my own hungry horror in her pretty eye, then I can bear the daily suck of hers. So I stood behind more curtains-plush dark velvet ones this time, as soft as the lining of her mouth—and watched Brad accepted the prize on behalf of us both. In his acceptance speech he spoke of my great virtue, to care for a creature so mysterious and wanting, but failed to mention my frequent jokes of tearing her apart.

I think I love him a little bit, because I disgust him neither with my extreme giving nor my extreme distaste. He, like Brandon, wants to split and relieve me, and although I told him that I cannot; I am merely waiting my time.

She does not like him. When he draws near, her face becomes more churlish, garish, the kicked-in flat of her snout more prominent as she pulls on my nipple in the farce of feeding. She places one warm rough hand, finger nubs spread distinctly, on the curve of my breast. This is why I must feed her outside; he does not like sand in his shoes, and watches instead from the glass door. I try to forget him, watch her face sweetening as she sucks light and gentle like a lover, but sometimes I am distracted, instead, by the crash of waves and how I could move my hips to that rhythm, his cock in me as keen and sharp as my nipples, the salt on my lips. I was distracted by such reveries on Monday, and so she turned herself into a narrow green and yellow bug. Her hard body—winged, suspended between six black legs sharp-angled—sprung to lift angry in the air.

She's been gone longer than ever before; all week I have had little to do. Brandon slipped a puppy care manual into a dog bowl, also a rubber kong and a short purple leash with a note that I have yet to read. He slipped this gift beside me as I sat on one of Kid Kare's battered fold-out tables, wondering if my boyfriend would forgive me. "She doesn't want a puppy," Brad muttered to Brandon. "She doesn't want to take care of anything right now."

"Listen," Brad said to me, "the baby might not come back. You might be done. Just check in once a week, see if she has returned, but otherwise you are free to go."

His eyes are brown or green, reflective and beguiling as her pink eye. My milk let down, flooding the thin cotton of my t-shirt with warmth.

I swung down to leave, hot flaring wet between my thighs as I considered how best to frame my invitation. Then I saw her: a group of co-workers, women who resent me mostly but are themselves as tired, had crowded quietly about her, noting any damage or change. I knew she wouldn't like that, so I came to her, as I always do.

She gave me her most dogged face, vivid and clashing. "We found her in a window," a woman told me quietly, knowing better than Brad or Brandon the complications of my disappointment. I stroked the baby's orange cheek, murmured to her; she knew as well as the woman, if not better, how my heart sunk at the sight of her, yet moved still by strength or duty to sustain.

I cajoled her, rocked her, sung to and stroked her; slowly her face eased, turned coyly into her dirty bonnet to reveal the inevitable pink of her eye.

I did not study my reflection there, already knowing as she knew. Instead I turned her from me, her boneless back tucked warm to my chest, bound firm in the steady of my forearms. I began to rock, breathing long and slow as I did, inhaling to lean back, exhaling to rock forward; together we moved over the pendulum of my waist, our chests rising, sinking in tandem as breath by breath we orchestrated our heartbeats back to dream-slow synch.

From the UV Files

File #132
MARY SHANLEY

Bullet in his Head

he walked around the city
for thirty-five years
with a bullet in his head
but it wasn't until he went
to the hospital for a cat scan
that the doctors discovered it.
when he was informed
he laughed it off.
said it must have happened
when he was crazy on drugs.
said it must have happened
when the streets were wild
with colors and energy.
said he thought he felt
something crossing Grand Street
one overwhelming night,
but he ignored it.
hurtled forward by the forces
of an unbridled life,
he had no time
to stop and explore
what might have caused
the sting in his scalp.

From the UV Files

File #133
RON D'ALENA

Skintight

He sits at the end of the bar
drinking coffee,
eating a Reuben sandwich,
crinkled wax paper face upturned toward hanging tvs:
one eye on NASCAR the other on People's Court.

Door opens: momentary sheet of sunlight.
On the blvd.: jack hammering, honking horns.
A guy comes in, sits down.
Whiskey/water.

Wax paper says,
    "Hate the smell of whiskey.
    When I was a teenager, a truck driver gave me a 5th of
Seagrams.
    Drank it all.
    Stumbled home through the snow.
    Daddy went running down to the truck stop, asking for the
man.
    Everyone cleared out. The man was gone.
    Never had whiskey again.
    Beers. Not whiskey."

"No don't want no beer.
    Use to get silly drunk.
    One night said something and hurt my wife's feelings.
    Never drank again."

The guy drinks his whiskey, then says
"Your wife, she don't drink neither?"

"Passed on 23 years ago.
    Smoking.

Tried to quit in '63. Withdrawals were cruel so I stopped bugging her
>Should have helped more.
>She was the woman for me.
>My brother-in-law, he's been married 7 times.
>Now he's back with the 4th because she's the mother of most of his kids
>and because of sex."

Commercials flicker.
No reason to stop talking.
>"Lived longer than I should have.
>Daddy died at 45 from a heart attack.
>Granddaddy died in his 50's from gangrene
>after snapping his leg
>while breaking a horse.

>"You know, I broke my arm in 11 places
>when I was 9 from playing baseball on a dirt road
>littered with stones.
>Doctors were going to amputate. Momma said,
>'You're not making a cripple out of my boy.'
>They set the break.
>Funny thing, got the bill 58 years later.
>Told them I'd pay up if they sent my x-rays.
>Never heard back."

Wax paper looks at the bar door,
then back.
>"Miscalculated.
>You can see that, can't you?
>Ought to be dead by now. Outlived everything.
>No money for nothing."

"Life's become skintight.
>SKINTIGHT.
>You hear what I'm trying to tell you?"

From the UV Files

Commercials end.
Wax paper upturns to the hanging tvs,
sips coffee,
takes a bite of sandwich.

From the UV Files

File #136
SCOTT NEUFFER

Fateless (A Dream)

I met Maria on a bluff overlooking the sea. I had gone there to die, to sink the heavy sickness in my heart. But she emerged from the black rocks like a nymph, moving with the flexibility of fire, the liquid property of light and wind. Her wild beauty charged the air. It electrified the void I was near surrendering to, not negating the emptiness, but galvanizing it, setting it afire until it consumed all things in a sweetly burning sadness known as longing.

"Eh lo," she said. "What iz it you'rre doing up here?"

Her accent chimed and crinkled like fire, I remember. A shimmery voice in a dream.

"Um…" I fumbled, trying to conjure an answer, trying to deflect suspicion.

The image of a bird formed in my head.

"I'm bird watching," I said.

She looked at me with eyes that were like taut brown fireballs, pieces of fresh-dug earth, irradiated, made elastic.

She laughed. "I don't know what iz that."

Her syntax rang like some exotic melody of freedom.

"It means I'm watching different kinds of birds. Some in the trees over there."

I pointed east to a belt of oak that wound like a question mark through the coastal hills. "Now look at the beach. There are tons of 'em out there."

Indeed, great waves of seabirds were rising and falling on the sand. I began describing every kind of bird I had ever seen or knew about. What I didn't know, I made up. What I couldn't name, I named.

Within the womb of an hour, we had risen in love with each other. Against the sun's tawny light, we let bend and be fused the temporal fabrics of our disparate circumstances. From then on, days opened like fairy tales, and nights hummed with sweet purple things.

We were both students at the university. Between classes, we'd meet in the library and prolong the seconds our lips touched, absorbing each other's restless fire, expanding, strengthening with clean, clear power. In class, I constantly thought of her: the wild and static blackness of her hair, the freckles like sunspots on the smooth brown star of her face, the concentrated tenderness of her lips, the grounding curves of her body. But I dreamed of more than her physical person. Mysterious images bloomed in my head. I saw radiant nebulae floating through space, like the pulsating embers of a cosmic fire. I saw oceans of brilliant liquids, reds and yellows and blues, gushing over each other in ecstatic chaos, thick and opaque, then galvanized, coursing in long, translucent flutes of color. I saw vast blankets of mud, inflamed with sunlight, throbbing with bugs, worms, leeches. And I saw children barefoot, wind-driven, running through forests of phosphorescent green. Leaving tracks of fire in ground that purred.

Sitting in class, my dreams eventually settled around one image: a house I would build for her, a wooden house flexing in the wind.

I worked construction part-time and would come home caked in dust, eyes as red as beestings. I would take long, hot showers and let the sheets of scalding water slip down my skin, leaving a raw and pinkish pulp, itching for cool currents of air, electric with anticipation. I would dress myself in clean, crisp fabrics, comb my hair, wipe my teeth with a curl of synthetic mint. She already would be out of class, and I would meet her downtown.

In the evening, the street lights were like bouquets of cast-iron flowers, blossoms electrified. The storefronts were smooth and handsome, holding behind their windows softly lit display cases lined in velvet, sprinkled with jewelry, sweaters, shiny black boots. Between the street lights, the chic trees marked the way, their trunks bare and bone-white, attenuated, branches twisting into great fountains of silken leaves. The leaves themselves dropped diamond shadows on the cement before us, fragmenting the otherwise fluid paths of city light.

One night, Maria and I sat on the bottom lip of a large alcove, carved in the side of a tall stucco building. I smoked a cigarette, and she talked about her family in Peru. She described the simple beauty of her Spanish-style home, the slabs of white stucco, the ruffled terracotta tiling of the roof, the blades of palm flickering in the plum-colored twilight. Not unlike our California city. She described her family, each member a nuance of the other, all dissolving in the stretched liquid of memory. Peru was becoming a ghost. Her new reality sat beside her, its warmth tangible. She had decided to let the other go. She had decided to forfeit her home in lieu of the house I promised her. It would be a wooden house flexing in the wind. Perhaps a red house on a yellow hill against a blue sky.

"Gib me a smoke!" a voice bellowed.

Its owner was a large black man who had emerged from a nearby alley. His face was molten-black and leered with malevolence. His eyes were white stones that bulged from the sockets, cracked with redness. He wore a slippery-black running suit that was nearly indistinguishable from the surrounding darkness.

"Alright," I said, trying to dismiss the threat in his voice.

I handed him a cigarette. He looked at me in confusion.

"Got a light?" he asked, so loudly that I knew he was testing my response.

Then he looked at Maria. His eyes protruded further from the sockets. A sinister smile split his cheeks. I could tell how bad he wanted her, the thought of it stroking his lips like the tail of the devil.

There was a skip in the heartbeat of time. I could tell that somewhere this man had crossed a line and hadn't come back. I summoned the boldest look I could and offered the lighter.

When the man turned back to me, he must have found a strong posture of defiance because his aggression fizzled. His face turned fearful. Again he looked at Maria, but cautiously.

"Can I keep da light?" he asked, dumbly, like a kid caught in the act.

"Take it," I said, with an overtone of fierceness that finalized his weakness.

He walked away. He became a curiosity of the night, a stereotype of the darkness, something hard to follow in the city's unending maze...

*

Daylight had emboldened us. We'd wandered away from our usual restaurants and found ourselves in a run-down deli in a questionable part of the city. We ate big slabs of turkey on fresh sourdough; the meat soured in our stomachs. Back outside, the sun-fired air was reassuring, despite its taint of smog. Unable to retrace our steps home, we turned down an unfamiliar street that seemed to run in the right direction. We passed liquor stores with black-barred windows, then a brick building, possibly a school, crusted over in graffiti. We could see an intersection up ahead. A row of pastel-colored condos beckoned from the other side. We were almost there.

A man separated from the shadows of the school. He was short and dark-skinned and had a shaved head that shone in the midday sun. He wore a white tank top that exposed his muscular arms. On the right arm danced a tattoo of a blue cross.

"Giv me whatever you got in tha wallet," he said.

His eyes were squinting, riding on the wave of some inner chaos. A switchblade flashed from his pocket.

"Alright," I said, putting up my hands in surrender.

Maria clung to the alcove of my body. I reached around to my back pocket.

"See, I'm getting it," I said.

He snatched the wallet, flipped it open. His eyes narrowed even more.

"Esse, thiz all you gawt?"

My fear became anger. Raged pulsed in my fingers. He looked at Maria.

"You with thiz gringo?" he sneered, acknowledging the Hispanic tint of her skin.

I could sense his initial intention give way to something more formidable, some piece of racial moralism he'd picked up on the street like a hot coin. It grew and hissed in his breath.

"Puta!" he declared.

He grabbed Maria's wrist with one hand, while the switchblade came up beside her like a fanged serpent. He lunged at her the very moment my rage unleashed itself—my fist hooking him in the mouth as the knife flashed and Maria screamed. There was a blue cross dancing on dark skin. Sirens wailing in the distance. The man dropped the knife and ran. Maria crumpled in my arms. Her blood dripped the color of a nightmare. Then police officers were standing over us conversing in a language I couldn't understand…

*

Maria was fortunate: the knife had just grazed her throat; the cruiser had just turned up the street. It could have been otherwise. How easily it could have been otherwise. By the whim of some feebly motivated molecule, the stir of a meaningless heat, spun, careening, drawing out in cold blood a different conclusion. But the blood was warm, and its leakage not irreparable. The blood was brilliant in its senseless spilling. It flowed in my eyes like a tropical fire, like the violence of a tropic city seething with injustice. I felt its hot, sneaky weight. I bathed in the squirming snakes. My hatred grew like wings of shrieking steel…

*

I met Cain Wilmer in the student union. He was slight in stature, with greasy black hair and a thin goatee. He'd been standing by the reference desk handing out political literature when he saw me in line. I was there to buy some permit or another.

"You look like someone who knows what they want and don't want," he said.

He approached me with an air of purpose that seemed either feigned or too deliberate for someone his age. I guessed he was a freshman, although the ashen color of his skin reminded me of something spoiled in the cellar, starved of sunlight, as if he'd leeched out any native tint he might have been born with. His eyes, however, were clear and blue.

"Because guys like us are few and far between," he continued. "Just take a look around, and you'll see yourself surrounded by fuckups."

His profanity dislodged something in my brain. I looked around to see if anyone was offended, but I realized the stranger already had coaxed me out of line.

"A bunch of fuckups who want you to pay for their mistakes, who don't want you to get what you deserve… which is freedom."

This last word rung in my head like a hammer banged on the shining memory of Maria.

"Freedom from them, the parasites, and all their weight."

I looked at the green army jacket that hung on the narrow frame of his body. On one arm colorful insignia I couldn't quite decipher. Tight jeans tattered at the knees. Shiny black combat boots.

"What are you trying to persuade me of?"

His face changed, softened.

"Man, I'm not trying to persuade you of anything. I'm trying to protect your rights as a citizen of this once-great country."

He handed me a pamphlet entitled, "Decisions of a New America." Addresses, dates and times were bulleted on the inside flap.

"By the way, my name's Cain."

"I'm Michael."

We shook hands. His grip was weaker than mine, his wrist thinner.

"It's all there," he said, pointing to the pamphlet. "If you've had enough and want to make it right, come check us out."

*

City light was no longer beautiful. It looked and tasted like copper. The trees were shrunk like captives in a meaningless march. The industrial light reddened Maria's face as she walked beside me. I had made her come. I had shut down the questioning music of her voice. When she'd asked me what kind of student meeting was held so far off campus, I'd told her it was a subversive one, perhaps at odds with the college administration or some other state bureaucracy. I'd told her I could no longer stand by as others threatened our love, threatened the home we were building. When she'd countered that the group sounded too radical, possibly racist, and reminded me that she herself was a minority brought to the U.S. through a student visa program, I'd answered that the organization's only concern was to stop the advancement of a criminal-empowering agenda. I'd assured her that she would be appreciated, that her beauty alone would trump any possible animosity. My main interest, I'd told her, was about good and evil, and she undoubtedly was good.

Following directions on the pamphlet, we veered right into the hills above the city. The air turned softer, cooler. We walked through a neighborhood of smoothly shaped houses, slabs of pink and white stucco, and cubes of yellow light where windows had been cut in the thick walls. The diaphanous foliage of citrus trees glittered around each house. Unlike their city counterparts, these suburban trees stood vindicated in the cleaner air. Between their leaves hints of star. The magic hum of a luxury car. Street-lamps like lollipops.

"I could live up here," I said.

Maria nodded.

"Yo también."

The house was like the others but larger, more prolific in the use of stucco and tile: white stucco rising at least three stories high to a corniced roof of terracotta, split in cross-shaped turrets and studded with white gargoyles. From a single window on the third story issued a coppery light, which fell on a medley of trees in the front yard. The trees whispered suspiciously to the shrubbery, and the shrubbery mumbled something to the immaculate lawn as we moved towards the house's lofty entrance. Lifted on columns of the Corinthian order, the portico was shaped like the crown of a white almond. Papal. I pressed the lighted circle beside the door, which was double-wide and dense with darkness, yet hid a delicate texture on the surface of its wood. We could hear the bell tolling on the other side. Silence. Then the sound of footsteps. The door opened with heavy deliberation. Cain's thin profile stood against the coppery light inside. His head had been shaved, and his shorn skull seemed on fire.

"I know you?" he asked, his eyes moving from Maria to me.

"It's Michael. We met in the student union."

He stood rigid.

"Oh Michael, that's right. You were the only one who took my pamphlet."

He laughed, almost a snort, then stepped outside. He grabbed my hand and smacked it against his chest.

"How you doing, my man?" He turned to Maria. "Who's this?"

"This is my girl. I thought I'd bring her along."

"Shit, she'd be the only chick here."

I intuited his eyes moving up and down Maria's body.

"I kin go," she muttered. Her accent froze the scene like some shadowy tableau.

"No, they won't mind. Am I right, Cain?"

He turned to me with a sideways expression so finely

wrought, so expertly controlled, that any specific emotion was undetectable.

"Come in," he said in a flat tone.

*

We climbed a beautiful grand staircase of marble and bronze. But the elegance was lost on the second floor, where a dim hallway led to a musty corner. There was a single shuttered window. A spiral of iron rose sinuously to an unseen lair.

"They're all upstairs waiting," Cain said in the same flat tone, as he gripped the iron and whirled up in a clamoring flash.

I looked at Maria. My instincts were screaming. Something wasn't right. She told me this much with her wounded, obliging eyes.

"Let's go up," I said. I whispered: "If we don't like it, we can leave."

We, too, gripped the metalwork in our hands, feeling its cold, immovable axis, and we climbed in nauseous circles to the third and final floor...

*

Cain led us into a large study, where four young men sat in leather chairs facing each other. Their heads had been shaved and now blazed in the copper light of a tall lamp beside them, similar to the standing lamps I had seen downstairs in the lobby. Bookshelves loomed in the background, rows upon rows of leather-bound books, the fine print of their titles concealed in shadow. On the side wall a golden sconce cast light onto an oil still-life of overripe fruit, colors moldering. In the corner an antique globe tilted off-axis. The floor beneath was dark and dusty wood. The ceiling above was a vaulted curve with a silvery varnish. Three skylights were cut like claw marks in the metallic contour.

"This is Michael. And what's your name?" Cain asked, turning to Maria with a contemptuous grin.

"I'm...." she started, voice quavering. "I'm Maria."

Her accent aroused each face. Young faces where the natural ruddiness of youth had been leeched out, terrorized. Where the heads had knocked together and formed a pale vengeance in the skin. Freckles gone black. Eyes like gun-metal. Barren skulls smoking in the light.

"Where you from?" one kid asked, making squishing sounds as he moved around in his chair.

I nudged Maria, who already was buried under my arm. I felt compelled to keep the conversation going at all costs, to be as friendly as possible. I nudged her again.

"P... Pey ru," she stuttered.

As if in confirmation, the kid lowered his face in a cross-hatch of shadow and light, but kept the top of his eyeballs glaring at her, his mouth down-turning in wicked lines.

"Why would you bring her to our meeting?" he asked, in a tone so serious I thought he was joking.

"Come on, looks like you guys need a girl around."

Cain moved to the front of the group, faced us with folded arms. I felt I could take his narrow frame, the naked head, break them on my knee. But it was the gravity of his face that scared me. Unlike those I had encountered on the streets, whose violence seemed desperate and random, there was something in Cain's face that suggested slow and terrible calculation, something I hadn't seen days before in the student union, not even minutes before during his strange greeting at the door. It was like the demon glow of heated steel. A red-hot skeleton sealed in the thick walls of the house. Some cunning I couldn't understand but that I sensed him feeding in silence to his peers.

"What do your parents do, Cain?" I asked.

Standing speechless, he closed his eyes and drew a deep breath, as if trying to center himself.

"Why did you bring this foreign whore to my house?" he said, opening his eyes.

I felt all consciousness wither, all dream-matter sucked into the denseness of the house.

"What'd you say?"

"I asked you why you brought this foreign whore into my house."

His friends responded to the insult like a pack of hyenas, clicking their fangs and whining.

"Why would someone of your heritage show up here with a spic bitch and pollute the rest of us?"

His profanity dislodged something in my brain, hot and

sacred, rushing like lava. I started towards him, but Maria pulled me back.

"We'rr leaving!" she shouted.

As she turned me around, I could see the hyenas rising, glowering beneath their skulls, behind their leader.

"You're not going anywhere," Cain said.

*

We were running through hallways with no light and no exit. I found a door and kicked it into a thousand hairy pieces. Maria wept. I hissed and pushed her into the unknown space. She found the light—a shock of fluorescent white. Then a black labyrinth burned in a rectangle of red silk. It took a few seconds before we realized it was a Nazi flag hanging on the wall. The other walls of the windowless room had the same metallic varnish as the ceiling in the study. On one side a glass case held a cache of black rifles, at least a dozen of them, perfectly lined, like the neat products of some morbid proof. On the other side a pocket-door revealed a half-bathroom: pedestal sink, filigreed mirror, porcelain throne. What a find! What a sanctum! I pushed Maria inside and told her to lock the door. Then I was shattering the gun case with my bare hands, blood flinging on the silver walls, brilliant in its drip. I had one of the assault rifles in my grip and wheeled its barrel toward the smashed-in door...

*

A shot exploded through the metal room. My ears screamed. I felt a punch to the stomach, except cleaner, quickly passing through me. Then it was warm and tingling. Then aching. Then aching harder. With a gasp I fell to the floor. I saw Cain with a pistol, following me down. I saw his blue eyes, locked like a frozen sea. I knew then that he'd done this before. I could see it. Behind him, blooming like a ghostly flower, rose the image of a man he'd killed. A large black man in a running suit. They'd stood around him and beat his blood into the street with metal bats. They'd called him nigger and spat on his dying body. His blood still slipped and crackled over the nylon suit. Then another man. A short Hispanic man with a tattoo of a blue cross. His ghost rose beside the black man like a worm in plastic. They'd stabbed him in front of his own house. They'd chased him half a block first, but finally got him in his front yard. They'd called him spic and told him he was paying for the sins of his country. His blood still coursed through the frigid blades of grass.

And now, unsatisfied, they killed their own: this white man who'd betrayed them, and his girlfriend who represented the destruction of nations.

I felt Cain's shadow move over me. He kicked my wound, but the pain emptied itself on the floor, dissolved on the cold, hard stratum. The tracks of fire that were my mind, my memories, began unraveling from life's luminous concentration. Thoughts, feelings, languages scattered like shot-gunned birds, then faded at the touch of unfeeling fate.

But they didn't finish me.

"You're gonna live to see what happens to spics who fuck white men."

Maria! I heard the scuffle of her feet, and what could only be the sweet cacophony of her screams ringing the metal room. I opened my eyes. The expanse of floor was like a vitreous sea of blood. In the distance feet heaved and stomped, with incredible weight of presence, like giants battling over the red world.

"Maria," I whimpered.

"Michael!" she screamed.

She screamed so loud that it broke all the delicate nuances of her accent.

"S'what happens to spic bitches like you!" squeaked one of the assailants.

His voice was so high-pitched, so puerile, so incongruous with the act, that I almost didn't believe it was happening. It was unfathomable that such inflexible childishness could write our destruction. The sick irony knocked me out like a final blow to the head...

*

I was dreaming of outer space. Ice-pocked asteroids were flocking together in the darkness, caught in the pull of some arcane magnetism. And somewhere there was light. I could see it. The fire of love disembodied and drifting through space. I could reach out and touch it. It burned me with its consciousness, electric with thought. It filled me with its power, clean and clear, and I could do anything. I was free...

*

I awoke in a sea of my own blood. I heard her sobbing. I heard smacking sounds. Grunts, roar. I moved my head and saw her face cringed in pain, cringed sharper each time Cain thrust upward inside her. The hyenas were holding down her limbs, and her torso was spread open in the shape of a cross.

I felt love focus like a river. It flooded the confines of my body and lifted each dying cell on a cushion of air. I rose to meet the tight metal room, which now lay open in all its infinite intricacy. Its plains and curves and corners gleamed.

Cain turned; he saw me and jumped to his feet. But I leapt like a beam of light and sent my fist through his skull. He flickered and fell like nothingness to the floor. The animals released Maria and scrambled to their feet, but they found no ground. I moved easily between them, from one to the other, striking the throat and face in clean, calculated blows, until they were all dead...

*

I carried her body down the tortured iron, through the maw of the portico, out unto the womb of night.

"Don't leave me," she whispered, as blood congealed on my arms, her blood, my blood, messed together in dark purple.

I started to run. Her head fell from the crook of my arm and lolled against the night. I stopped and collected her body into all my being. My arms burned with the weight. I knew it was the only house I would ever build for her—this small space between my chest and arms, this pocket of purple blood. And I tried to live there with her, if only for a moment. But understand that the oceans of space were still calling me. They should have been calling us both, but she was to live on. She would find a new home.

From the UV Files

File #148
CATFISH McDARIS

Flying In The Talons

Time is a measurement,
a withered harvest of
man's wisdom, a dream
within a nightmare

It's said you never fully
appreciate life until
you've faced death

Fear is a tired joke,
ducks on an icy pond,
termites, a ripe banana,
four artichokes, a burnt
match, an empty bottle

A green lizard in the talons
of a Mexican eagle,
a bulldog with its teeth
buried deep in your ass.

File #149
ELLEN DENTON

Heart Made of Rain

Dorothy

Dorothy Levine did not hold the office of "Town Gossip" in Hungerspeak, Montana, but if the position had become available, she would have filled it admirably. Almost devoid of self awareness, her conversations were composed of external factors that, like circus acrobats, cart-wheeled their way by her in passing: a spate of stormy weather, a flier passing before her eyes proclaiming in bold, bright colors the items that would be on sale at the local market that week, or a random story, passed on hot-potato style, or spewed like vomit around town, about some tragedy or scandal involving another neighbor. Probably all small towns have people like this, but by and large, underneath it all, they're good at heart, and do a fairly good job of otherwise passing for human.

It was six twenty-five in the morning when Meagan opened her front door in response to her persistent knocking. Dorothy had composed her expression into one of earnest looking solemnity, but inwardly, she was eager and excited at the prospect of being able to deliver a juicy tidbit of bad news.

"There's been a plane crash. From what I heard, it's Ed Wilkins. Crashed his crop duster into the cemetery that fronts those hills right outside town. I just thought you'd want to know right away."

"Thanks Dorothy. I already heard the... news. May Huxtable called me about it a little while ago."

Dorothy's lower lip quivered slightly, but she did her best to hide her disappointment. She prattled on about the few gory details she'd been able to glean earlier from the gossip line until Meagan got her to detach herself from the front porch and go back home.

Meagan

By seven, Meagan was at the cemetery. She stood shivering in the early morning air behind the yellow tape, along with a few neighbors and curiosity seekers. She was close enough to make out the heap of twisted metal that had once been a plane. She looked away and up at the sky, still silvery in the west.

"Really something that he died right in a cemetery huh?"

Meagan turned around. It was Alice Fairfield, the Hungerspeak Savings and Loan bank teller.

"Yeah," was all she could think of saying in response.

"I heard something—I don't know if it's true. One of the firemen walked out here a while ago and told someone the plane crashed nose down right into the spot where his wife's grave is. How's that for creepy and eerie?"

Meagan felt slightly sick. "Yeah. Pretty strange, I guess." She turned back to the graveyard and stared at the still smoking wreck.

*

Meagan marched through her day like an automaton, while inwardly, the news of Ed's death moved through her like ripples in a lake around a single thrown stone. She took a few calls, made arrangements to have an old couch picked up for donation to the local thrift shop, and engaged in polite, social conversation with neighbors she encountered while running errands in town. She could hear and see people's mouths moving when they spoke to her, but the words were as empty and meaningless as electric car windows rolling up and down. Her own words back to them tasted like dust in her mouth.

She and Ed had history, over 20 years worth. She and her husband, and Ed and his wife Lisi, moved in different circles so hadn't socialized much beyond the occasional chit-chat at 4th of July town picnics, but when her own husband died 17 years ago, Ed, in acts of neighborly kindness, would often come by to help with chores like fixing a fence gate gone awry, hauling off brush from her property, or sometimes just sitting a spell with her on the front porch to talk. By chance, they had a number of shared interests in common; it turned out they were both amateur seascape artists, loved heavy metal rock (something which used to drive Meagan's husband crazy, and which Ed simply hid from Lisi, a prim, devout, little Christian woman), and both understood, and would often have a good natured laugh, about the Dorothy Levines of this world. There was never anything romantic between them; Ed loved his own wife as Meagan still loved her husband, but kindred spirits, they did become true and fast friends. It was five years after her husband's death that this all changed, and she ended up sitting on the prosecutor's side of the courtroom during Ed's criminal trial, averting her eyes from him and rigidly clenching her jaw in the suppressed, smoldering fury only a massive betrayal can induce.

Ed

"You know Ed, you're this town's one claim to fame. You never told me that there's a plaque dedicated to you in the town hall."

Ed turned his face away from Meagan, pretending interest in the moths swirling around the front porch light. "It was nothing."

"It wasn't nothing. It says you're a war hero. What did you do in the air force?"

"Same as what I do now; I was a paramedic. That silly plaque was for parachuting into enemy territory with a combat unit."

"Yes, aaaaaannnnnnd???"

"I got shot, but continued working with the wounded and saved a bunch of lives, got a few fancy medals for it and blah blah blah. So there you have it."

"Wow, pretty cool!"

Ed smiled at Meagan and shrugged. "Yeah, there just is no greater satisfaction than saving a life or helping someone. It's kind of been a life-long purpose for me. When I was a kid, my bedroom was a like a hospital for every sick or injured stray creature in Hungerspeak. I remember once, when I was six, there were these ants crawling around in some spilled ice cream on the sidewalk. I was looking at them through a magnifying glass, and noticed one of the ants was teetering, like it was dizzy or something, so I—"

Ed never got to finish the sentence about his efforts to save the ant, because Meagan had gotten the picture and was laughing so hard it brought tears to her eyes.

From the UV Files

*

Three years after Meagan's husband died, Ed, a senior paramedic with an emergency response service at the time, saved the life of her then thirteen year old daughter, Casey. A few years later, this incident would be the beginning of the end for him.

*

Casey had been walking alone in the rain, down Oldham road. A car came rocketing around a turn, hit her and sped off. She was left lying in a widening pool of rainwater and blood, awake, and gasping for every breath. To this day, it's not known who called 911. It was assumed the hit and run driver did it from a disposable cell phone in a momentary burst of guilt. An ambulance showed up minutes later, and had it not been for Ed, Casey would have died before even making it to the hospital. He stopped the bleeding, and since he knew her well because of his friendship with Meagan, held her hand for the entire ambulance ride there. She was awake and terrified, but over the oxygen mask covering most of her face, kept her eyes fixed on Ed's. She held his gaze as though that alone would keep her alive. In his usual professional and caring manner, he smiled encouragingly and assured her she would be fine, and she was. She got out of the hospital six weeks later, and with the resiliency of youth, recovered fully. She carried on with the business of being a teenager, including going through a phase when she was fifteen, as young girls often will, of wanting to be an actress or a model. Meagan had no words to express her gratitude to Ed for saving Casey. The loss of her own husband had shattered her; she did not think she could have survived the loss of her only child.

It was two years after the accident when Casey told Meagan about how Ed had molested her in the ambulance. She told about how he had put his hands under her shirt and down her pants on the way to the hospital.

Eight months later the case came to court. Ed had been out on bail during that time. He denied the charges, but Casey was convincing enough on the stand to bring a guilty ruling by the judge. She had no reason to make something like that up, especially about a man who had saved her life.

His lawyer trotted out a seemingly endless parade of character witnesses for him, and as he had no prior criminal history, and was a war hero, was given no jail time, just probation and was placed on the registers sex offenders list.

It was the end of his career as a paramedic. He took a job as a mechanic at his friend Joe's Garage, but his crime and conviction had been the biggest scandal to ever hit Hungerspeak, and like a contagious disease, disgust and censure of him, fueled by the Dorothy Levines of the town, spread, and Joe lost so much business by reason of having Ed employed there, that he had no choice but to finally let him go. Ed then did handy-man jobs here and there, but sometimes people were loath to have something as heinous as a child molester around, and work became harder and harder to come by.

In the months after the trial it was awkward for him to even walk through the town. Acquaintances who had once greeted him enthusiastically now nodded politely and turned away, or pretended to be looking elsewhere altogether when they passed him in the street.

He had many close friends who stood staunchly by him through the trial and afterwards as well, but even with them, it was like a broadax had slashed an unclosable rift between him and the world he had known. He would be sitting at a poker game with his buddies, cold brews and laughter shared all around, when some off-hand, humorous mention was made about one of their teenage daughters doing this or that, or some risqué joke would be told, and a momentary, uncomfortable silence would fall over the room like a pall. Slowly, over the months, visits and invitations from even his most verbal supporters and friends dwindled.

Hungerspeak had been his home and the home of his family before him. He had built his life here and did not want to leave, but after a year of increasing hardships following his trial, he knew he needed to start a new life elsewhere. Even with being on a sex offenders list, he thought if he moved out of state to a large, major city, he could live his life in relative anonymity. There would be more options to find work as well. Right now, most of their financial support was coming from Lisi's small, home-based catering business and their savings. In a city, he could get a job in a factory or as a mechanic. Full background checks were seldom done for positions like that. He might even be able to get work, or at least do some volunteer work, helping people at a senior care center where his conviction for a sex offense with a minor might not be a factor. His own two children were away at collage, so there would be no disruption of their lives or schooling a move like this could cause. Ed, for the first time in a year, saw a light on the horizon.

Lisi

Lisi refused to uproot and move. She cited the client base she had built up over the years in her business, her church groups, her long term friends, and her two sisters, both of whom lived in Hungerspeak. Ed's reasoning and pleas fell on deaf ears. She was adamant.

None of the excuses she gave were the main, real reason, but she would never admit her true motives. Although Ed denied repeatedly that he had molested Casey, Lisi was a devout, bible-thumping Christian and knew well the evil inherent in man. She never believed or forgave him for bringing such ignoble disgrace to the family, and wanted to get back at him for what he had done. She wanted him to continue to suffer. She wanted him to continue living in shame. She wanted him to shrink more and more into himself. She wanted him to burn in hell and his life to be hell on earth. Such motives as hers, full of malevolence and spite, were so socially unacceptable in themselves, and so inherently evil, that even though she sometimes glimpsed them, like road kill in a rear view mirror, she barely could admit even to herself that she had them, let alone tell Ed her true feelings. She did, however, never miss an opportunity to make a sly, covert remark that would remind Ed of what he had done.

In the world Ed and Lisi had grown up in, people seldom divorced, nor did a good man ever abandon his family or fail to support and protect them as long as he was able. Ed was one such good man. Eventually, he apathetically accepted the fact that any hope of having the life he once had was over. He had earlier been trained to fly single engine planes. There were many farms and ranches in the state, and he was able to get work as a pilot doing crop dusting, fly-over horse herding, and other such jobs. He kept to himself. He supported his family and saw to their needs. Sometimes, late at night, he would sit out on the front porch and gaze up at the parade of stars and constellations heroically poised in the dark, clear sky, and he would cry. A dutiful husband, he cared for Lisi at home around the clock when, twelve years later, she got cancer, which not long after, killed her.

Even when she was dying, she never forgave him.

And he never forgave her.

*

Meagan now stood in front of her window, the one that faced Dorothy Levine's house across the road, thinking about Ed's death that morning and repeating to herself over and over "what's done is done. I have to protect my own." She remembered, with a stab of pain, shame, and guilt, thinking those exact same words by this very window, so long ago now, and why.

Casey

About two years had passed since Ed's trial and conviction. By then, Casey was eighteen and would shortly be starting bookkeeper training at a school in the nearby town of Granville. The director of a small, private medical center in Hungerspeak, the one Casey was taken to when she had her accident, was a close family friend and had promised Casey a job in their finance department when she completed her training and returned.

On the night before she was to leave for Granville, she came into Meagan's room in the middle of the night, turned on the light and sat down on Meagan's bed. Meagan shot bolt upright, instantly awake, because Casey was crying copious tears. She was crying so hard as she spoke, that she almost choked over her words when she told Meagan what would end up being, next to the earlier news of her husband's death and Casey's accident, the worst thing she would ever hear for the remainder of her life.

*

"Aren't you glad? Isn't this heavenly?"

"What ist?..I mean is." Casey giggled at her mistake in the self-conscious way a fifteen year old often will.

"What ya mean what ist? What ya think you're holding in your hand there?" Now all three girls broke into gales of laughter. Casey then started coughing so hard she had to put down the smoldering joint she was holding into an ashtray and wait till she got her breath again.

"Oh this, yea, I am really glad you older-by-one-year, more "worldly" girls are here to show me the ropes." Casey started laughing again. Coughing. Laughing.

"Yes, me and Vanessa are sophisticated ladies of the world. Speaking of worldly, are you really serious about pursuing an acting career when you finish High School?"

"I am."

"Then start getting your name out there now. I've been thinking, with what happened to you earlier, you can turn that into money in the bank."

"What do you mean?"

"Well think about it for a minute. You had this accident that almost killed you, and a family friend, who was also an EMT type guy, saved your life. Booorrrriiiing. But what if you put an exciting and unique twist on that, something they could even make a movie about?"

"L like what?"

Well, for instance, a story about a war hero sexually abusing a near to death thirteen-year-old in an ambulance would give your name and face national celebrity, especially if it went to trial. It could make your name a household word, and you could use that exposure later when attempting to launch your career."

"But that didn't happen."

"So what?"

*

Casey was essentially a good-hearted girl, but was not the sharpest knife in the drawer and had a sheepish mentality. Between that and a cloudy dullness that had enveloped her thinking from several months of sustained drug use, she was easily swayed and eventually went along with this ridiculous and destructive plan. She rehearsed her story with her cohorts, practicing it over and over until she could tell it in a dramatic and believable way.

Stories of sexual crimes were a dime a dozen; every big city had their share, and it soon became obvious, after the trial had come and gone, that the accusation against Ed and subsequent court case would get no more than local and some minimal state coverage. By the time Casey was close to graduating high school, she also knew she was going to be a bookkeeper, not a movie star.

As is often the case with the harmful or stupid things people do, they're easier done than confessed to, so what she did carry away from the experience, which would be hers to keep, was a very guilty conscience.

Meagan talked with her well into the night about what had occurred. Casey felt better, and they agreed she would leave as planned for her training the following morning. Meagan assured her that while she was away at school, she would work out the best course of action to now take in regards to Ed and getting his false conviction remedied.

The next day, after Casey was gone, Meagan stood looking out the window, still numb with the news of the previous night and the realization of the past few years of hell Ed must have gone through since the first public telling of the lie. His career had been ended, his standing in the community destroyed, his life and personal relationships shattered. A minor version of that might occur with her own daughter now, and by extension to herself, once the truth came out. It could jeopardize Casey's chance of getting the job that awaited her, as it would make her look unstable, unbalanced and dishonest. There might even be legal trouble or a civil law suit by Ed's children due to the perjury she had committed. If nothing else, she would be remembered for bringing about prosecution against a beloved war hero by bearing false witness, and people in small towns had long memories.

As she gazed out the window, lost in her thoughts about this, the mail truck pulled up in front of Dorothy's house. Dorothy came outside and started eagerly bending the mailman Ralph Macafee's ear about something. Meagan decided then and there that what was done was done. She had to protect her own. With a decisive snap of a cord she lowered the blinds and turned away from the window.

*

That was so many years ago, and as of today, Ed was dead. Meagan figured it wouldn't help him any if she now finally told the truth. It would only make it worse for her and Casey that they both kept it hidden all this time.

From the UV Files

Hungerspeak

It took over a week for the debris from Ed's crash to be completely carted off. The broken remains of his wife Lisi were re-casketed by her family; the mahogany "Princess" model she'd originally been buried in was shattered to smithereens when the plane dove nose first into the gravesite. Ed was then interred beside her at a service that surprisingly, almost the entire town turned out for, as Ed, despite everything, had been remembered by many as a well-liked man and a war hero. The area of the couple's gravesite was then re-sodded over with a healthy mixture of Kentucky Blue and Red Top grass. By the following spring, it blended in with the rest of the Hungerspeak graves like a patch in a cemetery quilt.

From the UV Files

CONTRIBUTORS

Timothy Bearly

Timothy Bearly currently resides in Sandpoint, Idaho where he likes to eat worms and sing songs. According to his teachers he has an insubordinate attitude (because he raises questions). According to his family he is a communist (because he doesn't believe in laissez-fairy tales). According to his fundamentalists peers he is the antichrist (because he named his dog Darwin). Notwithstanding his frustration with the relentless and groundless ad hominem bombardment, he kind of enjoys his status as persona non grata; he contends that ostracism helps one to write unfettered. Ironically, personal attacks also inflate his ego; it helps him to realize that he is on the right track. He can be lambasted via email: thebearlys@hotmail.com

Gary Clifton

Gary Clifton, forty years a cop, has an M.S. from Abilene Christian University and has short fiction pieces published or pending on over twenty online sites. He's been shot at, shot, stabbed, sued, and often misunderstood.

Ron D'Alena

Ron D'Alena was born in San Francisco, earned an MBA at the University of San Francisco, and now lives in Southern Oregon with his wife and son. His work has appeared and is forthcoming in numerous journals and magazines, most recently: *Crannog Magazine, Slipstream, Underground Voices, Lowestoft Chronicles, Blue Crow Magazine, Criminal Class Review* and *EDGE*. He is a two-time *Glimmer Train* Finalist and nominee for the 2012 Pushcart Prize for fiction.

Cassandra Dallett

Cassandra Dallett lives in Oakland, CA. She is Mama Cass to four kids and two Pit bulls. When not working as a Nurse Aid or cooking for her army, she writes poetry. Cassandra has published in *Hip Mama, The Chiron Review, Bleed Me A River, Ascent Aspirations, Criminal Class Review, Nibble,* and *The Milvia Street Journal* among many others. Look for links on www.cassandradallett.com

From the UV Files

Daniel Davis
Daniel Davis was born and raised in Central Illinois. Currently, he is the Nonfiction Editor for The Prompt Literary Magazine. You can follow him at Facebook.com/DanielDavis05 or at his blogspot: www.dumpsterchickenmusic.blogspot.com

Ellen Denton
Ellen Denton has been published in *Underground Voices, You and Me, Things Japanese, Fed Caps Words about work, Greenprints*, a Redstone Media Group Inc. magazine, in the *Spruce Mountain Press* Anthology, Vampires 2, and a *Cost of Care Group* publication; she took 4th place (plus publication) in *Echoes of the right to god* international essay contest, honorable mention in "Reading Writers" suspense fiction contest, and short list of finalists for both the "Smories" international short story contest and PK 2010 Poetry competition. She is also a two time finalist (plus publication) in the Scinti story contest.

William J. Fedigan
William J Fedigan writes about who he is, what he knows and where he's been. Contact: wfedigan@aol.com

Phillip Gardner
Phillip Gardner lives in Darlington, South Carolina, where he writes stories and screenplays. His more recent stories have appeared in *Euphony, New Delta Review, LIT, Interim* and *Eclipse*. He is the author of two story collections, Somebody Wants Somebody Dead and Someone To Crawl Back To (Boson Books).

Steven Gulvezan
Born in Detroit, Steven Gulvezan has worked as a journalist and library director. He continues to live in the Detroit area with his wife, Karen and his dog, Yogi. His book, *The Dogs of Paris*, is forthcoming from March Street Press.

Jonathan Hine
Jonathan Hine has been writing poetry for the past 15 years in an ill-advised attempt to write out what William S. Burrows called the "Ugly Spirit." The results of this experiment are inconclusive. He is unsure whether his attempts are reinforcing or rooting out the menacing infestations of negativity that the Bhagavad-Gita labeled "dark inertia." Jonathan's book, *A Symphony of Hells*, is available at Lulu.com, Amazon.com, barnesandnoble.com, etc.

TT Jax
TT Jax is a parent, partner, mixed-media artist, and writer currently living in the Pacific Northwest by way of 28 years in the deep South. His work has been published under a whole zoo of pennames in a variety of literary magazines, including *Mudluscious*, *Specter Magazine*, *The Mom Egg*, *Educe*, and *HipMama*.

Beau Johnson
Beau Johnson lives in Canada with his wife and three boys. He has been published before, in the darker, seedier parts of town. However, it is on Tuesdays that he and his family travel back through time in an attempt to correct that which once went wrong.

D. Keramitas
D. Keramitas was educated at the University of Hartford, Sorbonne, and the University of London, and holds degrees in literature and law. He lives in Paris, teaching English and law in the French university system. His short fiction has been published in many literary journals. His story "The Art of Flight" won the Paynton Scholarship at the 2010 Paris Writers Workshop. In addition, he has worked as a film critic for both print and on-line publications, and is a contributing editor to Movies in American History (ABC-CLIO). He has recently completed his first novel.

William C. Kilby
W. C. Kilby is a writer and wanderer currently based in Central Appalachia. His house is small, but it has a great porch. His favorite answer is yes, and his favorite reason is kindness. He writes out of fear that someone worse might take his place if he stops.

Jo Neace Krause

Jo Neace Krause was born in Shoulder Blade, Kentucky. Her writings and essays have appeared in various literary journals such as *The Yale Review, Exquisite Corpse, Other Voices, University of South Caroline Review, Web del Sol*, and other places. After winning a creative artist fellowship, she attended Ohio State University. She lives in Duck River in Hickman County, Tennessee.

Sara Letourneau

Sara lives in southeastern Massachusetts, where she works as a full-time technical editor and thrives as a full-time music lover, poet, and overall admirer of creativity. Since August 2008, she has also been a freelance reviewer for the Sonic Cathedral WebZine, which covers female-fronted rock and metal bands. Her poetry has appeared in The Curry Arts Journal and the anthology More Great Writing By People You've Never Heard Of. You can visit her blog at http://saraletourneau.wordpress.com/

Steven Loton

Steven Loton writes stories that are being published here and there. You can catch his writing around various lit mags across London, the UK, worldwide and in certain parts of the Galaxy; or find his blog at http://flamethrowingtheshortstory.blogspot.com.

Catfish McDaris

Catfish McDaris has been active in the small press world for 20 years. After 3 years G.I. Joe, he hopped freights & hitchhiked across the U.S. & Mexico. He built adobe houses, tamed wild horses, made cattle troughs, worked in a zinc smelter & painted flag poles. He lived in a cave & wintered in a Chevy in Denver. He ended at the post office in Milwaukee. A catfish farm is next, he hopes.

Nick Medina

Nick Medina is a young author from Chicago, Illinois. Since 2009 he has been published in print, online and audio formats by magazines, journals and short story anthologies in the United States and the United Kingdom. To read more of Nick's work, or to contact him with questions and comments, visit his website at:

From the UV Files

https://sites.google.com/site/nickjmedina/

Scott Neuffer
Scott Neuffer is a staff writer for The Record-Courier in Gardnerville, Nevada. His work has appeared in the *Nevada Appeal, Tahoe Daily Tribune, Carson Valley Almanac, Listen Magazine, Fiction Fix,* and the *Nevada Review.*

Ken Poyner
Ken Poyner has been knocking about the small press world for forty years, with latest appearances in *Corium, Menacing Hedge, Poet Lore, Subliminal Interiors, The Adirondack Review, Full of Crow* and several dozen other places. He lives with his power lifter wife and five rescue cats in the lower right hand corner of Virginia.

Christian Riley
Beginning at 5:00 a.m., Chris spends the only available lot of solitary time he gets in a day feeding his addiction to writing. If he's lucky, he'll get two hours in before "they" wake up, after which he lives a wonderful life as a family man and special education teacher. His stories have been accepted at a number of publishers including *Cover of Darkness, Midwest Literary Magazine, Bete Noire,* the *Absent Willow Review, Underground Voices, Residential Aliens,* and *Bards and Sages Quarterly.* You can reach him at his static blog: frombehindthebluedoor.wordpress.com.

Mary Shanley
Mary Shanley is a poet/writer who lives in NYC. She has had two books published: Hobo Code Poems and Mott Street Stories and Las Vegas Stories. She reads new work online, as well as publishing online.

Riley Spilman
Riley Spilman is a poet, student, and avid news-reader. When not found wasting his time on board games or science fiction, he wanders around cities looking for inspiration in whatever form it might take. His poetry focuses on the beauty and intricacies of language as well as the struggle for human decency when society titters over the abyss.

From the UV Files

From the UV Files

From the UV Files

www.ingramcontent.com/pod-product-compliance
Lightning Source LLC
Chambersburg PA
CBHW032122090426
42743CB00007B/422